The Temper of Our Time

The Temper of
Our Time

by ERIC HOFFER

PERENNIAL LIBRARY
HARPER & ROW, PUBLISHERS New York

Chapter I originally appeared in *Harper's Magazine*, June, 1965.

Chapter II originally appeared in the *New York Times Magazine*, Oct. 24, 1965.

Chapter III originally appeared in the *New York Times Magazine*, Nov. 29, 1964.

1966, under the title "Making a Mass Elite."

Chapter IV originally appeared in *Holiday*, March,

Chapter V originally appeared in the *Saturday Review*, Feb. 1, 1966.

Chapter VI originally appeared in *Cavalier*, August, 1966, under the title of "Changes."

The Temper of Our Time was first published by Harper & Row in 1967.

First PERENNIAL LIBRARY edition published 1969 by Harper & Row, Publishers, Incorporated, New York, N.Y. 10016.

Library of Congress Catalog Card Number: 67-11326.

To Norman Jacobson

Contents

Preface

To KNOW the central problem of an age is to have our fingers on a thread of continuity through the welter of willful events and unforeseen crises. It is my assumption that the main difficulty and challenge of our age is drastic change—from backwardness to modernity, from subjection to equality, from poverty to affluence, from work to leisure. These are all highly desirable changes, changes that mankind has hoped and prayed for through the millennia. Yet it is becoming evident that, no matter how desirable, drastic change is the most difficult and dangerous experience mankind has undergone. We are discovering that broken habits can be more painful and crippling than broken bones, and that disintegrating values may have as deadly a fallout as disintegrating atoms.

The essays in this volume try to make sense of some of the happenings of our time, and they all are concerned with aspects of change. Most of the writing also deals with the role of the intellectual, and in one place I suggest that our age is the age of the intellectual. Actually, it can now be seen that the intellectual who during recent decades aspired to ride and command the process of change in various parts of the world is one in a line of aspirants waiting to take their turns in the arena. Just now in Africa and elsewhere the intellectual is being elbowed out and supplanted by soldiers who will use armies rather than mass movements as instruments of change. It is significant that the American Negro's passage from inferiority to equality is proceeding more equably and effectively in the U.S. Army than anywhere else. The Army is at present the only place where the Negro is a human being first and only secondly a Negro. So, too, in Israel the army has been an unequaled agency for the conversion of polyglot immigrants into self-respecting Israelis.

It is conceivable that eventually other agencies powered by other human types are going to have their turn. The actors will come and go, but the arena and the menacing problem will remain the same.

E.H.

San Francisco, California
July, 1966

The Temper of
Our Time

1   *A Time of Juveniles*

THERE WAS A WEEK several years ago during which the newspapers reported an epidemic of student riots spreading from Istanbul to Teheran, Bombay, Saigon, Seoul, Tokyo, and Mexico City. Most of the riots had an anti-American flavor. And I remember how, early one morning, while waiting for the bus that would take me to the waterfront, I saw the headline of still another riot, and heard myself snorting with disgust: "History made by juvenile delinquents!"

The sound of my words had a peculiar effect on me. Inside the bus I did not look at the newspaper but sat staring in front of me.

Who makes history? Is it the old? How much of a role do the young play in shaping events? Things were coming together in my mind. I remembered that years ago I had inserted in *The Passionate State of Mind* an aphorism which read: "History is made by men who have the restlessness, impressionability, credulity, capacity for make-believe, ruthlessness and self-righteousness of children. It is made by men who set their hearts on toys. All leaders strive to turn their followers into children." This insight which came to me from observing two willful godchildren in action had been filed away in my mind and had not affected my thinking. Now it seemed to me that we can hardly know how things happened in history unless we keep in mind that much of the time it was juveniles who made them happen.

Until relatively recent times man's span of life was short. Throughout most of history the truly old were a rarity. In an excavation of one of the world's oldest cemeteries, the skeletons showed that the average age of the population at death was twenty-five, and there is no reason to suppose that the place was unusually unhealthy. Thus it seems plausible that the momentous discoveries and inventions of the Neolithic Age—the domestication of animals and plants; the invention of the wheel, sail, and plough; the discovery of irrigation, fermentation, and metallurgy—were the work of an almost childlike population, and were perhaps made in the course of play. Nor is it likely that the ancient myths and legends, with their fairy-tale pattern and erotic symbolism, were elaborated by burnt-out old men.

The history of less ancient periods, too, reveals the juvenile character of their chief actors. Many observers have remarked on the smallness of the armor which has come down to us from the Middle Ages. Actually, the men who wore this armor were not grownups. They were married at thirteen, were warriors and leaders in their teens, and senile at thirty-five or forty. The Black Prince was sixteen when he won fame in the battle of Crécy, and Joan of Arc seventeen when she took Orléans from the English. Without some familiarity with the juvenile mentality and the aberrations of juvenile delinquency it would be difficult to make sense of the romanticism, trickery, and savagery which characterized the Middle Ages. The middle-aged were out of place in the Middle Ages; troubadours and chroniclers gave them no pity and no mercy. Nor did things change markedly in the sixteenth century. Montaigne tells us that he hardly ever met a man as old as fifty. Salvadore de Madariaga says of Spain's great age (1550-1650) that in those days "boys of fifteen were men; men of forty were old men." He adds that when the dramatists of that age designated a man as old they meant a man of about forty—yellow-skinned, wrinkle-faced, and toothless. In the first half of the sixteenth century, Charles the Fifth became Emperor at the age of twenty, Francis the First became King of France at twenty-one, and Henry the Eighth King of England at eighteen.

The question is whether the juvenile mentality is confined to adolescents. Do people automatically grow up as they grow older? Is not juvenility a state of mind rather than a matter of years? Are there not teenagers of every age? In 1503 Cardinal Giuliano della Rovere was elected Pope at the age of sixty. He took the name of Julius the Second in honor of Julius Caesar, whom he esteemed as the greatest man who ever lived, and whose career he determined to emulate. So on the threshold of old age he put on a helmet and cuirass, mounted a horse, and set out to become a conqueror. Clearly, the juvenile mentality may persist or re-emerge in later life, even in old age.

In all times there are people who cannot grow up, and there are times when whole societies begin to think and act like juveniles. The twentieth century in particular has seen juvenilization on an almost global scale. No one can fail to discern the juvenile character of Communism, Fascism, racism (Ku Klux Klan), and the mass movements erupting at present in the underdeveloped parts of the world. Almost all the leaders of the new or renovated countries have a pronounced juvenile element in their make-up.

Arthur Koestler suggests that there is in the revolutionary "some defective quality" which keeps him from growing up. The indications are, however, that the present trend toward juvenile behavior has been gathering force for over a century and has affected people who cannot be classed as revolutionaries. Such behavior was rampant on the frontier and in the gold-rush camps, and the American go-getter, though he has no quarrel with the status quo, is as much a perpetual juvenile as any revolutionary. Militant nationalism, too, though not primarily revolutionary in character, fosters juvenile manifestations in all sorts of people. Laurens Van der Post calls nationalism "the juvenile delinquency of the contemporary world." Clearly, the juvenile pattern is not confined to people with "some defective quality" which keeps them from growing up, but may arise or be induced in all types.

To understand the process of juvenilization we must know something about the genesis of the juvenile mentality in the adolescent. We shall not get anywhere by looking for differences in the brain structure or the nervous system between adolescent and adult. I know of no demonstrable differences. The reasonable approach is to assume that the adolescent's behavior is induced largely by his mode of existence, by the situation in which he finds himself. This would imply that adults, too, when placed in a similar situation would behave more or less like juveniles.

Now, the chief peculiarity of the adolescent's existence is its in-betweenness: it is a phase of transition from childhood to manhood, a phase of uprootedness and drastic change. If our assumption is correct, other types of drastic change should evoke a somewhat similar psychological pattern. There should be a family likeness between adolescents and people who migrate from one country to another, or are converted from one faith to another, or pass from one way of life to another—as when peasants are turned into industrial workers, serfs into free men, civilians into soldiers, and people in underdeveloped countries are subjected to rapid modernization. One should also expect active people—whether workingmen, farmers, businessmen, or generals—who retire abruptly, and even women undergoing a change of life, to display proclivities and attitudes reminiscent of juveniles.

Let us have a close look at the experience of change. After the Second World War backward countries in Asia and Africa began to modernize themselves in an atmosphere charged with passion and a deafening clamor. As a naïve American I asked myself why the sober, practical task of modernization—of building factories, roads, dams, schools, and so forth—should require the staging of a madhouse. In *The Ordeal of Change* I tried to find answers to this question. My central idea was that drastic change is a profoundly upsetting experience, that when we face the new and unprecedented our past experience

7

and accomplishments are a hindrance rather than an aid. What Montaigne said of death is also true of the wholly new: "We are all apprentices when we come to it." We are misfits when we have to fit ourselves to a new situation. And misfits live and breathe in an atmosphere of passion. We used to think that revolutions are the cause of change. Actually it is the other way around: change prepares the ground for revolution. The difficulties and irritations inherent in the experience of change render people receptive to the appeal of revolution. Change comes first. Where things have not changed at all there is the least likelihood of revolution.

Now the fact is that the staging of a madhouse in the process of modernization is not peculiar to backward countries in Asia and Africa. Long before the present awakening of backward countries we had been living in an apocalyptic madhouse staged on a global scale by Germany, Russia, and Japan, which set out to modernize themselves at breakneck speed. Moreover, the mass movements, upheavals, and wars which are a by-product of change indicate that there is more to the experience of change than a state of unfitness, that the process involves the deeper layers of man's soul. After all, change such as the world has seen during the past hundred and fifty years is something wholly unprecedented and unique in mankind's experience. From the beginning of recorded history down to the end of the eighteenth century the way of life of the average man living in the civilized centers of the earth had remained substantially unchanged. To the Arab historian Ibn Khaldun it was self-evident that "past and future are as alike as two drops of water." The technology developed during the Late Neolithic Age lasted almost unchanged down to the industrial revolution. A greater gulf lies between us and Washington than lay between him and the Egyptian farmers who labored for Cheops. It would be legitimate, therefore, to assume that there is in man's nature a built-in resistance to change. It is not only that we are afraid of the new, but that deep within us there is the conviction that we cannot really change, that we cannot adapt ourselves to the new and remain our old selves, that only by getting out of our skin and assuming a new identity can we become part of the new. In other words, drastic change creates an estrangement from the self, and generates a need for a new birth and a new identity.

9

And it perhaps depends on the way this need is satisfied whether the process of change runs smoothly or is attended with convulsions and explosions.

It is of interest to have a quick look at the means employed by changeless primitive societies to tackle the one critical change no society can avoid: namely, the change from childhood to manhood. In the Congo, boys at the age of fifteen are declared dead, taken into the forest and there subjected to purification, flagellation, and intoxication with palm wine resulting in anesthesia. The priest-magician (nganga) who is in charge teaches them a special language, and gives them special food. Finally come the rites of reintegration, in which the novices "pretend not to know how to walk or eat and, in general, act as if they were newly born and must relearn all the gestures of ordinary life."* In several Australian tribes the boy is taken violently from his mother, who weeps for him. He is subjected to physical and mental weakening to simulate death, and is finally resurrected and taught to live as a man.

* Arnold van Gennep, *The Rites of Passage* (Chicago: Phoenix Books, The University of Chicago Press, 1960), p. 81.

The interest of these rites is in their motif of rebirth rather than in any bearing they may have on change in a civilized society. In the modern world change overtakes a whole population, and the denouement is not a return to an immemorial way of life. Here the sense of rebirth and a new identity is created by mass movements, mass migrations, or by a plunge into the perpetual becoming of sheer action and hustling. One becomes a member of a glorious Germany, a glorious Japan, a nation of heroic warriors destined to conquer the world; or one joins a revolutionary or religious movement which envisages a new life and one sees oneself as one of the elect marching in the van of mankind; or one actually immigrates to a new country and becomes a new man. Thus a time of drastic change is likely to become a time of wild dreams, extravagant fairy tales, gigantic masquerades, preposterous pretensions, marching multitudes with banners waving and drums beating, messiahs bringing glad tidings, and mass migrations to promised lands.

The tale of Moses and the Exodus is a luminous example of the difficulties encountered, and the outlandish means that have to be employed, in the realization of drastic change. Moses wanted to accomplish a relatively simple thing: he wanted to transform the enslaved Hebrews into free men. But, being a genuine leader, Moses knew that the task of endowing liberated slaves with a new identity and immersing them in a new life was not at all simple and required the employment of extravagant means. The Exodus from Egypt was the first step. But more vital was the fiction of a chosen people led by a mighty Jehovah to a promised land—the kind of milieu essential for a drastic human transformation.

Now, the human transformation which took place during the last hundred years was not the turning of slaves into free men but drastic changes brought about by the Industrial Revolution; yet here, too, the sense of rebirth and a new life was generated by exoduses (mass migrations), the fiction of a chosen people (nationalism), and the vision of a promised land (revolutionary movements). It is fascinating to see how in Europe during the second half of the nineteenth century the wholesale transformation of peasants into industrial workers gave rise not only to nationalist and revolutionary movements bringing the promise of a new life, but also to mass rushes to the new world, particularly the United States,

where the European peasant was literally processed into a new man—made to learn a new
language, adopt a new mode of dress, a new
diet, and often a new name. One has the impression that immigration to a foreign country was more effective in adjusting the European peasant to a new life than migration to
the industrial cities of his native country. Internal migration cannot impart a sense of rebirth and a new identity. Even now, the turning of Italian and Spanish peasants into
industrial workers is probably realized more
smoothly by immigration to Germany and
France than by transference to Milan and
Barcelona. So, too, the Negro who comes
to New York from the West Indies adjusts
himself more readily and smoothly to the
new life than the Negro who comes from the
South.

The juvenile, then, is the archetypal man in
transition. When people of whatever age
group and condition are subjected to drastic
change they recapitulate to some degree the
adolescent's passage from childhood to manhood. Even the old when they undergo the
abrupt change of retirement may display juvenile impulses, inclinations, and attitudes.

13

This is particularly true in this country, where leisure is not an accepted component of the active life. Thus retired shopkeepers and farmers have made Southern California a breeding ground of juvenile cults, utopias, and wild schemes. The Birch movement with its unmistakable flavor of juvenile delinquency was initiated by a retired candy maker and is sustained by retired business executives, generals, and admirals.

The significant point is that juvenilization inevitably results in some degree of primitivization. We are up against the great paradox of the twentieth century: namely, that a breakneck technological advance has gone hand in hand with a return to tribalism, charismatic leaders, medicine men, credulity, and tribal wars. The tendency has been to blame the machine. There is a considerable literature on the barbarizing and dehumanizing effects of the machine: how it turns us into robots and slaves, stifles our individuality, and dwarfs our lives. Most of the indictments of the machine come of course from writers, poets, philosophers, and scholars—men of words— who have no first-hand experience of working and living with machines. It should also be noted that long before the advent of the machine age the typical intellectual looked upon common people who did the world's work as soulless robots and automated ghouls. It is true that in the early decades of the Industrial Revolution, when men, women and children had to be dovetailed with iron and steam, the factories were agencies of dehumanization. But we of the present know that communion with machines does not blunt our sensibilities or stifle our individuality. We know that machines can be as temperamental and willful as any living thing. The proficient mechanic is an alert and intuitive human being. On the waterfront one can see how the ability to make a fork lift or a winch do one's bidding with precision and finesse generates a peculiar exhilaration, so that the skilled lift driver and winch driver are as a rule of good cheer, and work as if at play. Even if it were proven beyond a doubt that the assembly line makes robots of workers it still affects only a small fraction of the population, and cannot be held responsible for the nature of a whole society.

No, it is not the machine as such but drastic change which produces this social primitivism. The rapid urbanization of untold millions scooped off the land has been the central experience of our age, and the need of these uprooted millions for a new identity has generated and shaped the temper of our time. Whatever the means employed to satisfy this need, the result will be some degree of primitivization. Where a new identity is found by embracing a mass movement the reason is obvious: a mass movement absorbs and assimilates the individual into its corporate body, and does so by stripping the individual of his own opinions, tastes, and values. He is thereby reduced to an infantile state. This is what a new birth really means: to become like a child, and children are primitive beings—they are credulous, follow a leader, and readily become members of a pack. Immigration produces a similar reaction. Like a child the immigrant has to learn to speak, and how to act and assert himself. Finally, primitivization also follows when the search for a new identity prompts people to be eternally on the way by plunging into ceaseless action and hustling. It takes leisure to mature. People in a hurry can neither grow nor decay; they are preserved in a state of perpetual puerility.

But is social primitivization a fortuitous, unfortunate by-product or does it have some sort of a function in the process of change?

What is it that a society needs above all when it has to adjust itself to wholly new conditions? It needs utmost flexibility, a high degree of human plasticity. Now, a population juvenilized and primitivized, whether by a mass movement, mass migration, or immersion in ceaseless hustling, tends to become a homogeneous, plastic mass. We who have lived through the Stalin-Hitler era know that one of the most striking functions of a mass movement is the inducement of boundless human plasticity—the creation of a population that will go through breath-taking somersaults at a word of command, and can be made, in the words of Boris Pasternak, "to hate what it loves and love what it hates."

The True Believer is, then, a plastic human type thrown up by a century of ceaseless change. The adaptation to change has also produced the American hustler, a type as juvenile, primitive, and plastic as the True Believer, but functioning without ideology and the magic of communion. The immigrant, too, having been stripped of his traditions and habits, is easily molded. Finally, there is the plastic type of the warrior. All through history, conquerors have learned more willingly and readily from the conquered than the other way around. The conqueror does not see imitation as an act of submission and proof of his inadequacy. It is a fact that nations with a warrior tradition, such as the Japanese and the inheritors of Genghis Khan in Outer Mongolia, find the transition of modernization less difficult than nations of subjected peasants such as Russia and China. There is thus a kernel of practicalness in the preposterous tendency of an Indonesia or an Egypt to cast its people in the role of warriors. It is also plausible that the defeat of forty million Arabs by tiny Israel is rendering modernization of the Arab world more difficult and painful.

The throes of the machine age stem, then, not from the machine as such but from the social dislocation caused by the rapid urbanization of millions of peasants. It was this abrupt change in the life of the European masses in the second half of the nineteenth century which released the nationalist, revolutionary, and racialist movements that are still with us. A similar change in the backward countries of Asia, Africa, and Latin America is now setting off the social tremors that keep our world in a state of perpetual shock.

Where large-scale urbanization of peasants

has taken place without industrialization, the social consequences have been equally explosive as we have seen in recent decades in Latin America. In largely nonindustrial Argentina, Chile, Cuba, Uruguay, and Venezuela, townsmen already outnumber countrymen. Here rapid industrialization when it comes will find masses of urbanized peasants ready to be processed into factory workers, and the result is likely to be a considerable easing of social unrest rather than revolution.

The curious thing is that with the spread of automation we may see something like the present Latin American pattern emerging in the advanced industrialized countries. The banishing of workers by automation from factories, warehouses, docks, etc. will fill the cities with millions of unemployed workers waiting for something to happen. Condemned to inaction, and deprived of a sense of usefulness and worth, they will become receptive to extremism, and to political and racial intolerance. Thus it seems that in our present world problems come and go but the by-products remain the same, and the end of The Time of Juveniles is nowhere in sight.

2   *Automation, Leisure, and The Masses*

THE SPECTACULAR PROGRESS of mechanization on the San Francisco waterfront in 1963 filled me with foreboding.* It seemed to me that in almost no time the people I had lived and worked with all my life would become un-needed and unwanted. The newspapers and national magazines reinforced this impression. A leading manufacturer of automation equipment told a Congressional committee that already in 1963 automation was eliminating

* This chapter originally appeared in the *New York Times Magazine*, October 24, 1965.

40,000 jobs a week. *Time* magazine put the figure at 50,000. At the same time, in 1963, 2.5 million young people entered the labor market. It was estimated that 26 million young people would enter the labor market in the 1960s. Our economy had to create about 5 million new jobs a year in order to keep standing where it was, without touching the chronic pool of 5 million unemployed.

The assumption that once the economy started to grow at a satisfactory rate it would absorb most of the unemployed seemed fallacious. Eighty percent of the money spent on growth is spent on labor-saving devices. In 1963, it took a $30,000 increase in the gross national product to create one job. In 1953 it took $12,000; in 1973 it may take $75,000. No one expected our economy to grow faster than 5 percent a year. With a gross national product of $600 billion, 5 percent comes to $30 billion, and $30 billion creates only one million jobs. It did not seem, therefore, too farfetched to assume that in a matter of decades our cities would stand packed with masses of superfluous humanity. Now, at one point in history, God and the priests seemed to become superfluous, yet the world went on as before. Then again the aristocrats became superfluous and hardly anyone noticed their exit. In Russia, where they have capitalism without capitalists, businessmen are superfluous, yet things get done somehow. But when the masses become superfluous it means that humanity is superfluous, and this is something that staggers the mind.

In 1966 it is obvious that the great fear which possessed me in 1963 was not justified. There has been recently a sharp drop in the number of the unemployed, and even without a Vietnam emergency the consequences of automation are not likely to be as unprecedented and immediate as I had imagined. Some experts are now predicting that "Help Wanted" signs will soon be everywhere in evidence and unemployment down to the level of 2 percent. Nevertheless, the thoughts and musings set off by the doom-around-the-corner mood of 1963 have a validity of their own and are not affected by the course automation may take in the foreseeable future.

The thing that worried me about the prospective 20 to 30 million unemployed was not that they would starve. I assumed that the superfluous population would be given the wherewithal for a good living, even enough to buy things and go fishing. What worried me was the prospect of a skilled and highly competent population living off the fat of the land without a sense of usefulness and worth. There is nothing more explosive than a skilled population condemned to inaction. Such a population is likely to become a hotbed of extremism and intolerance, and be receptive to any proselytizing ideology, however absurd and vicious, which promises vast action. In pre-Hitlerian Germany a population that knew itself admirably equipped for action was rusting away in idleness, and gave its allegiance to a Nazi party which offered unlimited opportunities for action.

In this country, even the inaction due to retirement often becomes explosive. In Southern California, where retired farmers, shopkeepers, business executives, generals, and admirals abound, we have been treated to a madhouse of extremist cults, utopias, and movements. My feeling is that an energetic, skilled population deprived of a sense of usefulness would be an ideal setup for an American Hitler.

Yet it is part of the fantastic quality of human nature that the thwarted desire for action which may generate extremism and intolerance may also release a flow of creative energies. There are examples from every era illustrating this fact, and none more striking than the conditions which attended the first appearance of written literature in the ancient civilizations. We are often told that the invention of writing in the Middle East about 3000 B.C. marked an epoch in man's career because it revolutionized the transmission of knowledge and ideas. Actually, for many centuries after its invention writing was used solely to keep track of the intake and outgo of treasuries and warehouses. Writing was invented not to write books but to keep books. The earliest examples we have of writing are invoices and lists of articles. The scribe who practiced the craft of writing was a civil servant—a clerk and book-keeper. Literature was the domain of bards and storytellers who no more thought of writing down their stock in trade than other craftsmen would the secrets of their trade. Century after century the scribe went on keeping records. He felt smug in his bureaucratic niche, had no grievances and dreamed no dreams. Then, in every civilization, at some point, the scribe makes his appearance as a "writer." When you try to find out what it was that started the scribe "writing," the answer in every case is the same: the scribe began to write when he became unemployed.

In Egypt it happened toward the end of the third millennium B.C. during the breakdown of the Old Kingdom—the first catastrophic breakdown of civilization. The vast bureaucratic apparatus fell apart, and the scribe who had been so secure in his bureaucratic berth found himself suddenly abandoned, without status and without anything to do. We can hear an echo of the scribe's despair in two of the earliest fragments of Egyptian literature—"The Lamentations" of the former treasury official Ipuwer, and the former scribe Neferrohu. You can see how the scribe, deprived of his official identity, reaches out for a new identity—that of a sage, prophet, or national spokesman—and tries to shine again in the use of his skill with pen and ink by describing in sonorous phrases the evils which have befallen the land. We read how Neferrohu, "a scribe with cunning fingers stretched out his hand to the box of writing material and took him a scroll and pen-and-ink case, and then he put in writing." He wrote: "Up my heart that thou mayest bewail this land whence thou art sprung. . . . The whole land hath perished, there is naught left, and the black of the nail surviveth not what should be there."

In Sumer the oldest literary remains are from around 2000 B.C., after the fall of the Third Dynasty of Ur, "the most glorious age of Sumer." During the great age the scribes had other things to do. Sir Leonard Woolley expresses his surprise that the glorious Third Dynasty "left virtually no trace of any literary record." It was only when the great age was brought to an end by the invading Amorites and Elamites that the Sumerian scribes "took it in hand to record the glories of the great days that had passed away."

In Palestine written literature starts after the breakdown of the centralized Solomonic kingdom. The Phoenician traders next door had around 1000 B.C. perfected the simplified alphabet from the cumbersome picture writing of the Egyptians, and by adopting the new easy writing Solomon could turn a mass of illiterate Hebrews into proficient clerks to staff his vast bureaucracy. Even Amos, a sheep-herder from the village of Tekoa, could become a privileged clerk. And then Solomon dies and the whole thing falls apart. The army of new scribes find themselves suddenly

27

unemployed. Amos has to go back to his village and herd sheep again. It is not difficult to imagine his frustration and chagrin. You can see him back in Tekoa with his pen, inkstand, and papyrus roll declaiming on the evils which have befallen the land, and lashing out at the greedy traders and the corrupt officials and priests. He surrounds himself with a band of disciples whom he teaches to write, and who take down every word he says. Thus Amos establishes one of the most glorious literary traditions.

In Greece written literature makes its appearance after the breakdown of the highly bureaucratized Mycenaen civilization. Here, too, the introduction of the Phoenician alphabet increased the number of potential scribes who saw it as their birthright to regulate society yet could find no adequate employment. Hesiod, a contemporary of Amos, mastered the art of writing yet had to stay on the farm. He, too, was gripped with the impulse to exhort and instruct his fellow men, and to start writing.

In China written literature dates from the sixth century B.C., the chaotic period of "the contending states" which followed the dissolution of the Chou Empire. The country was full of roaming bands of unemployed scribes who went about arguing, philosophizing, intriguing, and writing. Confucius was of them. The hankering after a busy, purposeful life forced the energies of the disinherited scribes into creative channels.

Other examples, remote and recent, come to mind of the connection between forced inaction and the release of creative energies. Thucydides was a passionate general. He did not want to be a writer; he wanted to command men in battle. But after losing a battle he was exiled, and had to eat his heart out watching other generals fight the war. So he composed *The Peloponnesian War*, one of the finest histories ever written. Machiavelli was a born schemer. His ardent desire was to pull strings, negotiate, intrigue, caucus, go on missions, and so on. But he lost his job as a minor diplomat and had to go back to his native village, where he spent his days gossiping and playing cards at the village inn. In the evening he returned to his house, took off his muddy clothes, put on a toga, and sat down to write *The Prince* and *Discourses on Livy*.

One more example. During the reign of Louis XIV the French aristocracy produced a crop of remarkable writers: de Retz, Hamilton, Saint-Simon, La Rochefoucauld. If you ask why it happened in France and not in other countries, the answer is again—unemployment. While the aristocracies of England, Spain, Italy, and Germany were managing affairs, amassing fortunes, fighting wars, and even making and unmaking kings, the French aristocrats were taken off their estates, pulled out of the army, and brought to Versailles, where all they could do was watch each other and be bored to death.

Enough has been said to show that a loss of a sense of usefulness and a passionate desire for impressive action may release a creative flow in all sorts of people—in sheepherders, farmers, officials, generals, politicians, aristocrats, and run-of-the-mill clerks. It goes without saying that in addition to a thwarted desire for action there must be talent and a degree of expertise. People who have nothing to say or have no idea how to say it when they have something to say will not start writing no matter how optimal the conditions. La Rochefoucauld obviously had talent and, what is equally important, a taste for a good sentence. The reign of Louis XIV has been called "a despotism tempered by epigram," and La Rochefoucauld also had the salons in which expression was practiced as a fine art. We can, therefore, expect unemployment to release a creative flow in the masses only if we assume that the masses in America are not less endowed with genius than other segments of the population, and that it is possible to bring about a diffusion of expertise in literature, art, science, etc., comparable to the existing diffusion of expertise in mechanics and sports. I have always had the feeling that the people I live and work with are lumpy with talent. The cliché that talent is rare is not founded on fact. All that we know is that there are short periods in history when genius springs up all over the landscape, and long periods of mediocrity and inertness. In the small city of Athens within the space of fifty years there sprang up a whole crop of geniuses—Aeschylus, Sophocles, Euripides, Phidias, Pericles, Socrates, Thucydides, Aristophanes. These people did not come from heaven. Something similar happened in Florence at the time of the Renaissance, in the Netherlands between 1400 and 1700 during the great period of Dutch-Flemish painting, and in Elizabethan England.

What we know with certainty is not that talent and genius are rare exceptions but that all through history talent and genius have gone to waste on a vast scale. Stalin liquidated the most intelligent, cultivated, and gifted segment of the Russian population and made of Russia a nation of lesser mujicks, yet no one will maintain that Russia is at present less endowed with talent than it was before the revolution. I would not worry, therefore, whether the American masses have talents worth realizing. The possibility of a mass renaissance hinges thus on the feasibility of a mass diffusion of cultural expertise. My hunch is that such a diffusion could not be brought about without radical chances in our way of life. But of this later.

We know of one instance in the past where the masses entered the field of cultural creativeness as participators. We are told that Florence at the time of the Renaissance had more artists than citizens. Where did these artists come from? They were for the most part the sons of shopkeepers, artisans, peasants, and petty officials. Giotto and Andrea del Castagno were sheepherding boys, Ghirlandajo was the son of a goldsmith, Andrea del Sarto the son of a tailor, Donatello the son of a wool carder. Most of the artists served their apprenticeship with artisans and craftsmen. The art honored in Florence was a trade, and the artists were treated as artisans. They were dressed like artisans in long tunics with leather belts, and cloaks that came halfway down the leg. When Veronese was asked about his profession he answered: "I am a laborer" (Sono lavoratore). The sixteenth-century historian Bendetto Varchi expressed his surprise that the Florentines who had been accustomed from childhood to carry heavy bales of wool and baskets of silk, and who spent all day and a large part of the night glued to their looms, should harbor so great a spirit and such high and noble thoughts. Everyone in Florence seemed to know something about the procedures and techniques of the arts, and could judge whatever work was in progress. There was also a sort of spotting system. Just as in this country there is little chance that if a boy in a back lot throws a ball with speed and deftness the performance will go unnoticed, so in Florence there were discerning eyes watching the young for marks of talent. When a sheepherding boy picked up a piece of charcoal from the pavement and started to draw on the wall there

33

was someone who saw it and asked the boy whether he would like to draw and paint, and in this way Andrea del Castagno became a painter. It was, it is true, all on a small scale. But a big country like ours is after all made up of a large number of small social units.

Where the development of talent is concerned we are still in the food-gathering stage. We do not know how to grow it. Up to now in this country when one of the masses starts to write, paint, etc., it is because he happens to bump into the right accident. In my case the right accident happened in the 1930s. I had the habit of reading from childhood, but very little schooling. I spent half of my adult life as a migratory worker and the other half as a longshoreman. The Hitler decade started me thinking, but there is an enormous distance between thinking and the act of writing. I had to acquire a taste for a good sentence—taste it the way a child tastes candy—before I stumbled into writing. Here is how it happened. Late in 1936 I was on my way to do some placer mining near Nevada City, and I had a hunch that I would get snowbound. I had to get me something to read, something that would last me for a long time.

So I stopped over in San Francisco to get a thick book. I did not really care what the book was about—history, theology, mathematics, farming, anything, so long as it was thick, had small print and no pictures. There was at that time a large secondhand bookstore on Market Street called Lieberman's and I went there to buy my book. I soon found one. It had about a thousand pages of small print and no pictures. The price was one dollar. The title page said these were *The Essays of Michel de Montaigne*. I knew what essays were but I did not know Montaigne from Adam. I put the book in my knapsack and caught the ferry to Sausalito.

Sure enough, I got snowbound. I read the book three times until I knew it almost by heart. When I got back to the San Joaquin Valley I could not open my mouth without quoting Montaigne, and the fellows liked it. It got so whenever there was an argument about anything—women, money, animals, food, death—they would ask: "What does Montaigne say?" Out came the book and I would find the right passage. I am quite sure that even now there must be a number of migratory workers up and down the San Joaquin Valley still quoting Montaigne. I ought to add that the Montaigne edition I had was the John Florio translation. The spelling was modern, but the style seventeenth century— the style of the King James Bible and of Bacon's Essays. The sentences have hooks in them which stick in the mind; they make platitudes sound as if they were new. Montaigne was not above anyone's head. Once in a workers' barrack near Stockton, the man in the next bunk picked up my Montaigne and read it for an hour or so. When he returned it he said: "Anyone can write a book like this."

The attempt to realize the potentialities of the masses may seem visionary and extravagant, yet it is eminently practical when judged by the criterion of social efficiency. For the efficiency of a society should be gauged not only by how effectively it utilizes its natural resources but by what it does with its human resources. Indeed, the utilization of natural resources can be deemed efficient only when it serves as a means for the realization of the intellectual, artistic, and manipulative capacities inherent in a population. It is evident, therefore, that if we are to awaken and cultivate the talents dormant in a whole population we must change our conceptions of what is efficient, useful, practical, wasteful, and so on. Up to now in this country we are warned not to waste our time but we are brought up to waste our lives.

Does this mean that we have to eliminate or radically change our present free enterprise system? Not at all. On the contrary, the state of affairs we are striving for might actually give more leeway to the people who operate and benefit from the present system. For we shall free them from responsibility for the un-needed and unwanted millions who will re-move themselves to a place where they can experiment with a new way of life. In other words, we recommend here two social systems coexisting side by side, not in competition and strife but in amity and mutuality, and with absolute freedom of movement from one to the other.

Usually, when we try to think of a substitute for our present system, the choices which of-fer themselves are singly or in combination: society as a church, society as an army, so-ciety as a factory, society as a prison, and society as a school. For our purpose the choice must be the last named—society as a school. I am not unmindful of the fact that so far, except in science and philosophy, schools have not been a forcing house of talent. The best of our literature, painting, sculpture, music, etc. has not come out of schools. It is also true that as we look around us we find that the most oppressive and ruthless ruling classes in our present world have a large number of former schoolteachers. This is true of the Communist countries, of the new nations in Asia and Africa, and of the government by professors in Portugal. But we shall have to take the risk and provide against tyranny by schoolmasters.

I would start with a pilot state made up of a slice of northern California and a slice of southern Oregon, and run by the University of California. I would call it the state of the unemployed, and anyone crossing into it would automatically become a student. The state would be divided into a large number of small school districts, each district charged with the realization and cultivation of its natural and human resources. Production of the necessitites of life would be wholly automated since the main purpose of life would be for people to learn and grow. I said that the school districts would be small, for I am convinced that the unfolding of human capacities requires a social unit in which people of different interests, skills, and tastes know each other, commune daily with each other, emulate, antagonize, and spur each other. The absolute freedom of movement from one system to the other and from one district to the other will result in a continued sorting out of people, so that eventually each system and each district will be operated by its most ardent adherents.

I am convinced that the coexistence of two social systems in one country would enhance our sense of freedom. For freedom is predicated on the presence of alternatives in the economic, cultural, and political fields. Even in the absence of tyranny freedom becomes meaningless where there is abject poverty, political inertness, and cultural sameness. And certainly no alternative can be as productive of a sense of freedom as the alternative of two different social systems.

Finally, it would be particularly fitting if the new states of the unemployed were to be created in parts of the country that have been depleted and ravaged—where forests have been destroyed, mines worked out, the soil exhausted. The simultaneous reclamation of natural and human resources would add zest and a higher congruity to the new societies.

To sum up: The business of a society with an automated economy can no longer be business. The choice will be between a Great Society and no society at all; between a society preoccupied with the realization and cultivation of its human resources and a society in the grip of chaos.

The great fear which possessed me in 1963 made me do things I never dreamed of doing. After years of hardly ever sticking my nose outside the waterfront I found myself running around, shooting my mouth off, telling people of a turning point ahead as fateful as any since the origin of society, and warning them that woe betides a society that reaches such a turning point and does not turn. I also noticed, as the months went by, how myths and legends came floating into my mind. It was some time before I realized that the myths dovetailed into a pattern, that they were telling a coherent story—a version of automation. Here it is.

When God created the world He immediately automated it, and there was nothing left for Him to do. So in His boredom He began to tinker and experiment. Man was a runaway experiment. It was in a mood of divine reck-lessness that God created man. "In the image of God created He him," and it was a fore-gone conclusion that a creature thus made would try to emulate and surpass his creator. And, indeed, no sooner did God create man than He was filled with misgivings and sus-picions. He could not take His eyes off His last and strangest creation. I can see Jehovah leaning over a bank of clouds contemplating the strange creature as it puttered about under the trees in the garden of Eden, wondering what was going on in the creature's head—what thoughts, what dreams, what plans, and what plots. The early chapters of Genesis make it plain that God was worried and took no chances. The moment man ate from the tree of knowledge God had His worst fears con-firmed. He drove man out of Eden and cursed him for good measure.

But you do not stop a conspirator from conspiring by exiling him. I can see Adam get up from the dust after he had been bounced out, shake his fist at the closed gates of Eden and the watching angels, and mutter: "I will return." Though condemned to wrestle with a cursed earth for his bread and fight off thistles and thorns, man resolved in the depths of his soul to become indeed a creator—to create a man-made world that would straddle and tame God's creation. Thus all through the millennia of man's existence the vying with God has been a leading motif of his strivings and efforts. Much of the time the motif is drowned by the counterpoint of everyday life, but it is clear and unmistakable in times of great venturesomeness. In the fabulous Late Neolithic "when men began to multiply upon the face of the earth," and in a burst of creativeness invented the wheel, sail, plow, brickmaking, metallurgy, and other momentous devices, they also set out to build "a tower whose top may reach unto heaven." They said they were building the tower for the glory of it, to "make us a name," but God knew better. "Behold," He said to His retinue of angels, "this they begin to do, and now nothing will be restrained from them, which they have imagined to do." So He confounded their language and scattered them abroad upon the face of the whole earth. It was only six thousand years later that the modern Occident picked up where the builders of the Tower of Babel left off.

It was the machine age that really launched the man-made creation. The machine was man's way of breathing will and thought into inanimate matter. Unfortunately, the second creation did not quite come off. Unlike God, man could not immediately automate his man-made world. He was not inventive enough. Until yesterday, the machine remained a half-machine: it lacked the gears and filaments of will and thought, and man had to use his fellow men as a stopgap for inventiveness. He had to yoke men, women, and children with iron and steam. The machine age became an echo of the fearful tale of the Bull of Phalaris. This story tells of an Athenian artist who made a brazen bull for the King of Phalaris. The bull was so lifelike that the artist was seized with a desire to make the bull come alive and bellow like a real bull. Of course he was not inventive enough to do it, but he hit on the idea of using human beings as a stopgap. He constructed the throat of the bull so that when a human being was placed inside the belly and a fire lit underneath, the shrieks and groans of the victim as they came through the specially constructed throat sounded like the bellowing of a live bull. Even so during the past 150 years millions of human beings were scooped off the land and shoveled into the bellies of smoke-belching factories to make the Bull of Phalaris roar. There was no escape for the mass of people from the ravenous maws of factories and mines. If they crossed the ocean and came to America the factories and mines were there waiting to receive them.

Then yesterday, almost unnoticed, the automated machine edged onto the stage. It was born in the laboratories of technical schools where mathematicians and engineers were trying to duplicate the human brain. And it was brought into the factory not to cure the disease of work which has tortured humanity for untold generations, but to eliminate man from the productive process.

Power is always charged with the impulse to eliminate human nature, the human variable, from the equation of action. Dictators do it by terror or by the inculcation of blind faith; the military do it by iron discipline; and the industrial masters think they can do it by automation. But the world has not fallen into the hands of commissars, generals, and the National Association of Manufacturers. There is a change of climate now taking place everywhere which is unfavorable to the exercise of absolute power. Even in totalitarian countries the demands of common folk are becoming determining factors in economic, social, and political decisions. There is, therefore, a chance that the denouement of automation might be what we want it to be.

I shall not forget the day mechanization made its entrance on the San Francisco waterfront. Discharging newsprint used to be one of the hardest jobs. The rolls, some of them eight feet high and weighing almost a ton, were landed horizontally on a platform, rolled onto long-handled metal trucks, and then hauled away. You had to watch your step, strain every muscle to balance the load, and be continually on the run. Now the rolls come out upright, two at a time, and land themselves. The clamp bridle released the rolls automatically when they land. Then a special lift runs up, puts its padded arms gently round the two rolls, lifts them up like a feather, backs into the dock, and stacks the rolls two high when necessary. All that first day I watched the rolls come out. All I had to do was steady the rolls with a pat, and change the gear now and then. I said to myself: "The skirmish with God has now moved all the way back to the gates of Eden. Jehovah and his angels with their flaming swords are holed up in their Eden fortress, and we with our

45

automated machines are hammering at the gates. And right there, in the sight of Jehovah and his angels, we shall declare null and void the ukase that with the sweat of his face man shall eat bread."

Certainly, this mood was not shared by many of my fellow longshoremen. They displayed an instinctive wariness as if wanting to make sure the thing wouldn't bite them. This despite the fact that a contract with the employers protects us against a loss of earnings and against layoffs. In less-protected industries the reaction is probably more poignant.

The fact is that the mad rush of the last hundred years has left us out of breath. We have had no time to swallow our spittle. We know that the automated machine is here to liberate us and show us the way back to Eden; that it will do for us what no revolution, no doctrine, no prayer, and no promise could do. But we do not know that we have arrived. We stand there panting, caked with sweat and dust, afraid to realize that the seventh day of the second creation is here, and the ultimate sabbath is spread out before us.

3   *The Negro Revolution*

THE PLIGHT of the Negro in America is that he is a Negro first and only secondly an individual. Only when the Negro community as a whole performs something that will win for it the admiration of the world will the Negro individual be completely himself. Another way of putting it is that the Negro in America needs pride—in his people, their achievements, their leaders—before he can attain self-respect. At present, individual achievement cannot cure the Negro's soul. No matter how manifest his superiority as an individual, he cannot savor "the unbought grace of life."

The predicament of the Negro in America,

then, is that what he needs most is something he cannot give himself; something, moreover, which neither governments, nor legislatures, nor courts, but only the Negro community as a whole, can give him.

Despite the vehement protestations of Negro writers and intellectuals, the Negro is not the white man's problem. On the contrary, the white man is the Negro's chief problem. As things are now, the Negro is what the white man says he is—he knows himself only by white hearsay. That which corrodes the soul of the Negro is his monstrous inner agreement with the prevailing prejudice against him. To annul the white hearsay and be what he chooses to be the Negro must become his own playwright, stage his own play, and cast himself in a role of his own choosing. It must be a heroic play, staged in a part of the country where the Negro's wrongs are glaring, and the attempt to redress them attended with deadly risks. There are counties in Alabama and Mississippi where Negroes are a majority. If a single such country, preferably a small one, could be quietly organized to elect a sheriff and defend him against interference from the outside, there would be set in motion a course of events which could bring salvation to the Negro in every part of the country. It would be salvation by disciplined, controlled violence, with opportunities for magnanimity. If a Bull Conner or a Sheriff Clark comes to such a county he is disarmed, given a good lunch, and driven back to the county line. To say that the odds are enormous against such a staged small-scale Negro Alamo ending in success is beside the point. Defeat here would mean more in increments of Negro self-respect than any number of victories in New York and San Francisco. The Negro needs genuine, unequivocal heroes. Martyrs or slogan-slingers cannot make history. Surely, if in Israel a few thousand fugitives from gas chambers stood up on their hindlegs and defied forty million Arabs it should be possible for American Negroes to stand up to a pack of cowardly white trash. The black counties in Alabama and Mississippi are more truly the homeland of the Negro than Palestine is the homeland of the Jew. Yet one has the impression that the Negro has no taste for the patient, quiet organizational work which is the taproot of any durable social achievement. The prevailing feeling seems to be that everything the Negro needs must come full grown

from without. When James Baldwin went to
Israel several years ago there was something in
him that kept him from seeing what he should
have seen; namely, a paradigm of what the
weak can do to heal their souls. He wrote
instead an article for *Harper's* magazine in
which he said that a cynical Britain and a cynical America *gave* Palestine to the Jews. To
Baldwin it is self-evident that if you have
something it is because someone gave it to
you. He seems unaware of the elementary fact
that no one can give us freedom or take away
our shame and that all we can expect from
others is that they wish us well.

One begins to wonder whether the American
Negro has the capacity to create a genuine
community with organs for cooperation and
self-help. You strain your ears in vain amid
the present Negro clamor for a small voice
saying: "Leave us alone and we will show you
what we can do." If it be true that the only
effective way to help the Negro is to help him
help himself, then the Negro's aversion to,
or perhaps incapacity for, a self-starting, do-
it-yourself way of life makes it questionable
whether he can ever attain freedom and self-
respect. One cannot think of another instance
where a minority striving for equality has

been so deficient in the capacity for mutual aid and cooperation. Almost invariably when a Negro makes his mark in whatever walk of life his impulse is to escape the way of life, the mores and the atmosphere of the Negro people. He sees the Negro masses as a millstone hanging about his neck, pulling him down, and keeping him from rising to the heights of fortune and felicity. The welloff or educated Negro may use his fellow Negroes to enrich himself (in insurance, newspaper publishing, cosmetics) or to advance his career in the professions or in politics, but he will not lift a finger to lighten the burden of his people. Thus, the most enterprising and ambitious segment of the Negro population has segregated itself from the Negro millions who are left to wallow in the cesspools of frustration which are the Negro ghettos.

The Negro leaders seem to have little faith in the character and potentialities of the Negro masses. Their words and acts are largely directed toward non-Negro America. They are not aware of the Negro masses as a reservoir of power and as an instrument of destiny. And this lack of faith in the Negro masses is dictating the singular pattern of the Negro revolution. Its objectives, tactics, and finances are not predicated on massive Negro backing. A cursory check among my Negro fellow long-shoremen on the San Francisco waterfront (there are some 2,000 of them earning between $7,000 and $10,000 a year) showed that no one of those questioned has been asked to contribute to the Negro cause and not one of them has come near a CORE picket line, whereas many white longshoremen receive requests for money from Negro organizations, and some of them, and their daughters, are passionately involved in CORE affairs. Whether it be legitimate or not to expect as much from the Negro as we expect from ourselves, it is clear that we can expect little from the Negro so long as he does not expect much from himself.

Since the revolution has no roots in the Negro masses, it cannot grow. It cannot engage in long-range programs which after a period of maturing may yield an abundance of striking results. It goes for immediate, showy objectives. It operates wholly in the present, and has no thought of the future. In the past, wherever there were many wrongs to right, the one least capable of yielding palpable results was attacked first. In early nineteenth-century England the abuses which called for remedy were many. There was unimaginable poverty among the masses, and a lack of protection by law of the weak, yet the attack which rallied all the reforming forces was directed against parliamentary corruption. One has the feeling that the prospect of Negro equality would have been brighter had the first target been disfranchisement rather than segregation. But the Negro leaders, having no faith and no roots in the Negro masses, cannot wait for votes to yield results. They cannot heed Nkrumah's advice: "Seek ye first the political kingdom and all others shall be added unto it."

The questionable nature of the Negro revolution manifests itself in its choice of enemies. It wants an abundant supply of tame enemies —real enemies are too dangerous—and the way to come by tame enemies is to declare that your friends, the white liberals, are enemies because they are white. One can almost smell the psychological twist involved when a James Baldwin or a LeRoi Jones vilifies and baits white liberals who have championed the Negro's cause all their lives. So utterly convinced are Baldwin and Jones of the irremediable worthlessness of the Negro people that anyone who thinks well of the Negro must

53

seem to them simple-minded or simply dishonest.

By a similar twist the Negro revolution tries to obtain tame substitutes for its only legitimate battleground.* Until recently, the revolution has had no stomach for Mississippi and Alabama—except for occasional forays. Hence we find the head of CORE in San Francisco in 1964 announcing to the world, from the steps of the San Francisco City Hall, that San Francisco is Mississippi. The Reverend Galamison from New York, who on that day happened to be in our city, amplified the statement by saying that San Francisco is worse than Mississippi. Even Martin Luther King is reported to have said that the Negro's

* This chapter originally appeared in the *New York Times Magazine* in 1964, published there in slightly different form. I do not know whether the participation of the Negro masses in the civil rights movement has increased appreciably in the last two years. There is still no vivid awareness that genuine emancipation is a do-it-yourself job. There is still a shying away from quiet, patient organization, and a penchant for showy, quick results, and for tame enemies and tame battlegrounds. There is still the illusion that achievements are the echo of words. The present clamor for Black Power conveys the impression that power is something that comes in cans and all you have to do is reach out and grab it.

real problem is in the North and not in the South. In short, the voice of the Negro revolution is telling us day in, day out, without hesitation and without qualifications, that it is we outside the South who are the Negro's real enemies; it is we who oppress him, exploit him, and brutalize him.

How does this sound to our ears, and how does my kind of people react toward it?

The simple fact is that the people I have lived and worked with all my life, and who make up about 60 percent of the population outside the South, have not the least feeling of guilt toward the Negro. The majority of us started to work for a living in our teens, and we have been poor all our lives. Most of us had only a rudimentary education. Our white skin brought us no privileges and no favors. For more than twenty years I worked in the fields of California with Negroes, and now and then for Negro contractors. On the San Francisco waterfront, where I spent the next twenty years, there are as many black longshoremen as white. My kind of people does not feel that the world owes us anything, or that we owe anybody—white, black, or yellow—a damn thing. We believe that the Negro should have every right we have: the right to vote, the right to join any union open to us, the right to live, work, study, and play anywhere he pleases. But he can have no special claims on us, and no valid grievances against us. He has certainly not done our work for us. Our hands are more gnarled and workbroken than his, and our faces more lined and worn. A hundred Baldwins could not convince me that the Negro longshoremen who come every morning to our hiring hall shouting, joshing, eating, and drinking are haunted by bad dreams and memories of miserable childhoods, that they feel deprived, disabled, degraded, oppressed, and humiliated. The drawn faces in the hall, the brooding backs, and the sullen, hunched figures are not those of Negroes.

Equally absurd is the contention that the American Negro is alienated from America. Despite discrimination, the Negro actually seems more at home in this country than any other segment of the population. It is doubtful whether even the Negro intellectual could transplant himself and prosper. The white men who populated this continent, most of them peasants, were not of the type that transplant well. Their incurable homesickness not only made them perpetual wanderers but also gave them the feeling of being strangers on this planet; it drove them to impose their own man-made world on God's creation to a degree never attempted before, and undoubtedly contributed to America's unprecedented dynamism.

Even when it tries to be gentle, the voice of the Negro revolution grates on us and fills us with scorn. The Negro seems to say: "Lift me up in your arms. I am an abandoned and abused child. Adopt me as your favorite son. Feed me, clothe me, educate me, love and baby me. You must do it right away or I shall set your house on fire or rot at your doorsteps and poison the air you breathe."

To sum up: The Negro revolution is a fraud. It has no faith in the character and potentialities of the Negro masses. It has no taste for real enemies, real battlegrounds, and desperate situations. It wants cheap victories and the easy way. A genuine mass movement does not shy away from desperate situations. It wants above all to prove the validity and potency of its faith, and this it can do only by acting against overwhelming odds, so that whatever it achieves partakes of the miraculous. Indeed, where there are no difficulties the true revolutionary will deliberately create them, and it often looks as if the chief function of his faith is to get the revolutionary out of difficulties he himself created.

I have said that the Negro outside the South can have no special claims on us and no valid grievances against us. This does not mean that the Negro is not in real trouble and that he has no desperate problems which others do not have to face.

This country has always seemed good to me chiefly because, most of the time, I can be a human being first and only secondly something else—a workingman, an American, etc. It is not so with the Negro. His chief plight is that in America he cannot be first of all a human being. This is particularly galling to the Negro intellectual and to Negroes who have gotten ahead: no matter what and how much they have, they seem to lack the one thing they want most. There is no frustration greater than this.

Second, if every trace of discrimination were wiped away overnight, the Negro outside the South would still be in the throes of a soul-wrenching crisis, and we must know something of the nature of this crisis if we are to make sense of what is happening in the

Negro ghettos. The Negro writer Ralph Ellison has pointed out that the American Negro is now undergoing a double drastic change. By merely stepping across the Mason-Dixon Line he steps from feudalism into the maelstroms of industrialism, and from legal subjection to legal equality. Now, everything we have learned about the pains and difficulties inherent in an adjustment to the new underlines the enormous handicaps which beset the Negro in any attempt to begin a new life and become a new man. The Negroes who emigrate from the South cannot repeat the experience of the millions of European immigrants who came to this country. The European immigrants not only had an almost virgin continent at their disposal and unlimited opportunities for individual advancement but were automatically processed on their arrival into new men: they had to learn a new language and adopt a new mode of dress, a new diet, and often a new name. The Negro immigrants find only meager opportunities for self-advancement and do not undergo the "exodus experience," which would strip them of traditions and habits and give them the feeling of being born anew. Above all, the fact that in America, and perhaps in any white

59

environment, the Negro remains a Negro first, no matter what he becomes or achieves, puts the attainment of a new individual identity beyond his reach. Mr. Ellison describes the fantastic forms which the groping for a new identity often assumes in the bedlam atmosphere of the Negro ghetto: "Life becomes a masquerade, exotic costumes are worn every day. Those who cannot afford to hire a horse wear riding habits; others who could not afford a hunting trip or who seldom attend sporting events carry shooting sticks."

It seems doubtful, therefore, whether the Negro can adjust himself to a new existence as an individual on his own. He cannot cross alone the desert of transition and enter an individual promised land. Nor can he avail himself of a genuine mass movement to give him a sense of rebirth and sustain him until he can stand on his own feet. Up to now, America has not been a good milieu for the rise of a mass movement. What starts out here as a mass movement ends up as a racket, a cult, or a corporation. Unlike those anywhere else, the masses in America have never despaired of the present and are not willing to sacrifice it for a new life and a new world. In this, the American Negro, despite his handicaps, does not differ fundamentally from his fellow Americans. He has no extravagant dreams and visions, and no wild hopes. He cannot conceive of anything more grand and desirable than the life lived by a middle-class American. Another way of putting it is that the American Negro minority is more American than minority. It cannot generate the alchemy of the soul which enables "the weak things of the world to confound the things which are mighty . . . and things which are not to bring to nought things that are." Like his fellow Americans, the Negro sets his heart not on "things which are not" but on things he sees in store windows. Hence, when Negro masses act, you have looting orgies and not a mass movement. It is questionable, therefore, whether it will be a mass movement that would cure the "nowhereness" and "nobodyness" of the Negro ghetto and lead the Negro out of the present crisis.

But what of Elijah Muhammad and the Black Muslim movement? Alone of all the Negro leaders Elijah Muhammad has a vivid awareness of the vital need of a new birth in any drastic human transformation, and he alone has mastered the technique of staging a new identity. In one sense the Black Muslim movement is trying to do to the Negro what America automatically did to the millions of immigrants from Europe. By joining the Nation of Islam the Negro is stripped of his habits, attitudes, opinions, beliefs, etc. He is given a new name, a new religion, and a new way of life. He is processed into a new man. That in order to do this Elijah Muhammad had to concoct doctrines of breathtaking, almost insane, absurdity should not come as a total surprise to anyone aware of the fantastic quality of man's nature. Often in human affairs the simplest ends can be reached only by the most roundabout and outlandish means. And the fact is that the Black Muslim movement can point to many solid achievements. It has transformed idlers, criminals, junkies, and drunkards into clean-living, purposeful human beings.

Yet it is highly doubtful whether in this country the Nation of Islam could ever become a movement of powerful sweep and drive. America is simply not favorable for the unfolding and endurance of genuine mass movements. The enormous digestive and assimilative capacity of this country is nowhere demonstrated more strikingly than in what it has done to mass movements. It has made of

Puritanism a forcing house of successful capitalists; it turned Mormonism into a school for business tycoons; and even American Communism is becoming a preparatory school for successful real-estate dealers.* And now the Black Muslim movement is becoming Americanized: it is equipping its converts for success in practical affairs. If Elijah Muhammad or his successor has vision, he will realize that the future of his movement lies not in America but in Africa. It is conceivable that an Islamic heresy hatched by Negroes, preaching the primacy of the Negro race, and coupled with American industrial knowhow might become an unequaled instrument of empire in Africa. It confined to America, the Black Muslim movement may eventually become a holding company of stores, banks, factories, and farms. The most it could aspire to would be a miniature Utah with a mosque in its capital of New Mecca.

As to the other black nationalist groups which are springing up across the country, they are manifestations of the Negro's passion for alibis and the easy way out. They are a plunge toward the impossible to escape the

* On the San Francisco waterfront the Communists are the most effective capitalists.

arduous effort required to attain the possible. As a black nationalist all you have to do is shoot your mouth off about the fire next time, and about grabbing six or seven Southern states, founding a Negro empire and breathing down the neck of a cornered, frightened white America. Your heart swells with heroic négritude, and you don't have to lift a finger to do a thing.

Finally, I cannot see how the American Negro can escape the crisis of identity by identifying himself, in the words of Martin Luther King, "with his black brothers of Africa and his brown and yellow brothers of Asia, South America, and the Caribbean." Assuming, as I must, that the American Negro is as American as I am, I cannot see at present in the whole of Asia, Africa, and Latin America a single achievement, a single personality even, to inspire me with wholehearted admiration, to set my heart and mind on fire, and prompt me to identify myself with it. It is possible to see how a James Baldwin or a Malcolm X, lusting for a taste of power, can identify himself with a pseudointellectual dictator like Nkrumah. But it is inconceivable that a Negro longshoreman should swell with pride at the

64

thought of a megalomaniac pie-card who fancies himself a lord of creation.

Surely, it should be the other way around: it is the American Negro who should demonstrate to the world what Negro energy, initiative, skill, and guts can do, and serve as an object of identification for Negroes everywhere. It is to the American Negro that the new Negro nations of Africa should be able to turn when they want to build factories, dams, and railroads, or create an army, or start an irrigation system. Again one cannot help thinking that what a handful of Jews in Israel have done for the self-respect of Jews everywhere, and what they are doing to help new nations in Asia and Africa, should not be so utterly beyond the reach of twenty million American Negroes who breathe the air we breathe and share in the work we do.

The question remains: What can the American Negro do to heal his soul and clothe himself with a desirable identity? It has to be a do-it-yourself job. Anything done to and for the Negro must be done by Negroes. There cannot be a non-Negro Moses leading Negroes to a promised land. Non-Negro

America can offer only money and goodwill. As we have seen, the Negro cannot look for a genuine mass movement to lead him out of the frustration of the Negro ghettos, nor can he attain self-respect by an identification with Negroes and négritude outside America. What, then, is left for him to do?

The only road left for the Negro is community building. Whether he wills it or not, the Negro in America belongs to a distinct group, yet he is without the values and satisfactions which people usually obtain by joining a group. When we become members of a group, we acquire a desirable identity, and derive a sense of worth and usefulness by sharing in the efforts and the achievements of the group. Clearly, it is the Negro's chief task to convert this formless and purposeless group to which he is irrevocably bound into a genuine community capable of effort and achievement and which can inspire its members with pride and hope.

Whereas the American mental cimate is not favorable for the emergence of mass movements, it is ideal for the building of viable communities; and the capacity for community building is widely diffused. When we speak of the American as a skilled person we have in

mind not only his technical but also his political and social skills. Once, during the Great
Depression, a construction company that had
to build a road in the San Bernardino Mountains sent down two trucks to the Los An-
geles skid row, and anyone who could climb
onto the trucks was hired. When the trucks
were full, the drivers put in the tailgates and
drove off. They dumped us on the side of a
hill in the San Bernardino Mountains, where
we found bundles of supplies and equipment.
The company had only one man on the spot.
We began to sort ourselves out: there were so
many carpenters, electricians, mechanics,
cooks, men who could handle bulldozers and
jackhammers, and even foremen. We put up
the tents and the cook shack, fixed latrines and
a shower bath, cooked supper, and next morning went out to build the road. If we had to
write a constitution we probably would have
had someone who knew all the whereases and
wherefores. We were a shovelful of slime
scooped off the pavement of skid row, yet we
could have built America on the side of a hill
in the San Bernardino Mountains.

I have no way of telling whether two
truckloads of Negroes would have performed
as well. What I know is that the distance be-

tween the average and the exception is greater in a Negro than in a white group; and it is plausible that a Negro group might have needed an injection of leadership from without to get organized. This suggests that the mobilization of Negro energies is hardly conceivable without the reintegration of the Negro middle class with the Negro masses.

When I speak of vigorous Negro communities, I do not mean Negro ghettos. You can have an effectively functioning Negro community even when its members live anywhere they please. What I have in mind is Negro centers, societies, agencies, loan associations, athletic clubs, discussion clubs, and the like. You can see such communal organs functioning among the Jewish, Japanese, Chinese, and other minorities. My feeling is that right now the Negro in San Francisco, and probably elsewhere, is ripe for some grand cooperative effort. It could be the building of a model Negro suburb, or a Negro hospital, a Negro theater, a Negro school for music and dance, or even a model elementary or trade school. You need dedicated men and women to mobilize and canalize abilities and money toward a cherished goal. It is being done in America every day by all sorts of people. Someone has to start these things—a single individual or a small group. In San Francisco the two thousand affluent longshoremen could be such a group.

The healing of the Negro by community building will be a slow process, and the end results, though a durable source of pride and solid satisfaction, will not be heavenly. There is no heaven on earth and no promised land waiting for the Negro around the corner. Only the rights and the burdens and the humdrum life of a run-of-the-mill American.

4   A Name For Our Age

THE GENERAL IMPRESSION seems to be that the age in which we live is the age of the masses. Half the time when you open a book or start a discussion you find yourself dealing with mass production, mass consumption, mass distribution, mass communication, mass culture, mass this and mass that. We blame the masses for all our ills: for the vulgarization of our culture and politics, for the meaninglessness of our way of life and, of course, for the population explosion.

Actually, America is the only country in which the masses have impressed their tastes and values on the whole of a society. Everywhere else, from the beginning of time, societies have been shaped by exclusive minorities of aristocrats, scribes, businessmen, and the hierarchies of sacerdotal or secular churches. Only in America did the masses have a chance to show what they could do on their own, without masters to push them around, and it needed the discovery of a new world to give them the chance. But in America just now the masses are on their way out. With the coming of automation 90 percent of the common people will become unneeded and unwanted.

Nor is there room any longer for the special aptitudes and talents of the masses. There was a time in this country when the masses acted as pathfinders and pioneers. They plunged into the unknown, cleared the land, built cities, founded states, and propagated new faiths. The masses built America and for almost a century shaped its future. But it is no longer so. America's future is now being shaped in fantastically complex and expensive laboratories manned by supermen, and the masses are on the way to becoming a waste product no one knows what to do with.

No. Our age is not the age of the masses but the age of the intellectuals. Everywhere you look you can see intellectuals easing the traditional men of action out of their seats of power. In many parts of the world there are now intellectuals acting as large-scale industrialists, as military leaders, as statesmen and empire builders. By intellectual I mean a literate person who feels himself a member of the educated minority. It is not actual intellectual superiority which makes the intellectual but the feeling of belonging to an intellectual elite. Indeed, the less valid his claim to intellectual superiority the more typical will be the intellectual. In Asia, Africa, and Latin America every student, every petty member of the professions, and every clerk feels himself equipped for national leadership. In Britain and Western Europe the intellectual, though not as assertive in claiming his birthright to direct and order society, nevertheless feels far superior to the practical men of action, the traditional leaders in politics and business. In the Communist countries the intelligentsia constitutes the ruling class.

In America the educated have not until recently developed a clear-cut, unmistakable intellectual type. There has been a blurring of types in this country. The differences are relatively slight between the educated and the uneducated, the rich and the poor, the old and the young, civilians and soldiers. It is remarkable how many topics there are—sports (including hunting and fishing), cars, gadgets, diets, hobbies, the stock market, politics—in which Americans of all walks of life are equally interested and on which they can all talk with some expertise. The paradox is that it is this sameness which gives to every human type in this country a striking singularity in the eye of the foreign observer. When Edmund Wilson went to London some years ago the British intellectuals could not believe their eyes: Edmund Wilson looked like a businessman. In 1963, a delegation of American longshoremen to Latin America found it hard to convince local labor leaders that they were bona fide workingmen. To a foreign observer, the American businessman is classless; "grandee, entrepreneur and proletarian all in one."*

The American intellectual has not always been what he is now. When you read what New England intellectuals were saying about common people early in the nineteenth cen-

* Richard Hertz, *Man on a Rock* (Chapel Hill: The University of North Carolina Press, 1946), p. 28.

tury you are reminded of what British and
French colonial officials were saying about the
natives when the clamor for independence rose
after the last war: "Wait and see what a mess
these savages will make of things."

A resemblance between intellectuals and colonial officials strikes us at first sight as in-
congruous. We associate colonialism with
soldiers and businessmen. I remember how
when I first read about the Italian Catholic
hierarchy in northern Europe during the late
Middle Ages, I was struck by how much it
resembled a colonial regime. There was a con-
tinuous flow of tribute from the North, and
cushy jobs for young Italians. It reminded me
of the relations between Britain and India in
the heyday of the British Raj. I saw the Reformation as a colonial revolution, and it
seemed to me quite logical that it should have
fostered national as well as religious separa-
tism. Luther was a colonial revolutionary. "In
the eyes of the Italians," cried Luther, "we
Germans are Teutonic swine. They exploit us
like charlatans, and suck the country to the
marrow. Wake up, Germany!" Though I knew
that the hierarchy of the Catholic Church was
made up of intellectuals, it did not occur to

75

me at the time that here was an example of colonialism by intellectuals. I could not connect intellectuals with colonialism.

With the lessons of the present before our eyes we know better. We know that rule by intellectuals—whether by an intelligentsia in a Communist country, by native intellectuals in the new countries, or by professors in Portugal—unavoidably approaches a colonial regime. This is a colonialism that begins at home. Hence, too, the obvious fact that the liberation movements in Asia and Africa which were initiated and won by native intellectuals, have resulted not in democratic governments but in a passage from colonialism by Europeans to colonialism by natives. The typical intellectual everywhere is convinced that common people are unfit for liberty and for self-government. It is instructive to read what Patrice Lumumba wrote about the African masses before he became Saint Lumumba. In his book *Congo My Country,* written before Congo's independence, Lumumba proposed to the Belgian rulers that they assimilate the African intellectual and together form an elite. As to the masses: "The status quo would be maintained for the uneducated masses who would continue to be governed and guided, as in all countries, by the responsible elite—the white and African elite."

What does an economy run by intellectuals look like? It is colossal: big plans, big statistics, gigantic steel plants, factories, dams, powerhouses—the biggest ever! The intellectual cannot be bothered with the prosaic business of producing food, clothing, and shelter for the people. He wants to start at the end and work backward. He pants for the grandiose, the monumental, and the spectacular. Though factories, dams, etc. are practical things, the intellectual sees them as symbols of power and lordship rather than means for utilitarian ends. In Russia they build the biggest steam shovel ever made, while everywhere in the country you see people carrying brick and mortar on wooden platforms, four men lifting at four corners, because there are neither buckets nor wheelbarrows. It would be hardly possible to make sense of rule by intellectuals without taking into account their consuming passion for grandeur. "The human heart," wrote D. H. Lawrence, "needs, needs, needs splendor, gorgeousness, pride, assumption, glory and lordship. Perhaps it needs these more than it needs love; at least even

77

more than bread." Though the intellectual has been preaching the primacy of economics in the historical process, he shows an aristocratic disdain for economic law. He wants to make history himself and let economics catch up the best way it can. Listen to Doctor Sukarno: "How do we become a great nation? Do we need only rice and bread? A nation does not live only on rice and bread. A nation with a flaming spirit is a great nation. Our food is spirit."

In politics, the intellectual who as a "man of words" should be a master of the art of persuasion refuses to practice the art once he is in power. He wants not to persuade but to command. We now realize that government by persuasion has been an invention of the traders rather than of the educated. The trader is usually more interested in the substance of power than its appearance. The intellectual wants not only to possess power but to seem powerful. Of what avail is the possession of power if you have to argue and persuade? Moreover, the intellectual is not satisfied with mere obedience. He wants to obtain by coercion a response as fervent and acclamatory as that obtained by the most effective persuasion. Silence is subversive—the womb of yet unborn cries of rebellion. Thus soul raping has become a feature of government by intellectuals. Euripides did not know the whole story when he said, "A slave is he who cannot speak his thoughts." We now know that a thousand times more a slave is he who is not allowed to keep silent.

It is significant that there should be so many schoolmasters in the ruling intellectual elites. The passion to teach is far more powerful and primitive than the passion to learn; and for all we know the passion to teach may have been a crucial factor in the rise of the revolutionary movements of our time. Now and then, when I look at Russia, Asia, and the new Africa it seems to me that a band of maniacal schoolmasters have grabbed possession of half of the world and turned it into a vast schoolroom with millions of cowed pupils cringing at their feet. This unprecedented infantilization of whole populations has been one of the most fateful consequences of the intellectual's coming to power. It is partly responsible for the primitivization of the social structure—the return to tribalism, medicine men, and charismatic leaders—which in a large part of the world is going hand in hand with rapid technological modernization. These builders of a heaven on earth have made a nightmare of the words of Jesus that "whosoever shall not receive the kingdom of heaven as a child shall in no wise enter therein." And it is in this nightmare that the schoolmaster's wildest dream is coming true: when he speaks the whole world listens. And how these schoolmasters do talk! Four-hour speeches, six-hour speeches—a schoolmaster's heaven.

In international affairs the coming of the intellectual has brought to the fore the cult of naked power. To an intellectual in power liberalism, the readiness to compromise, and moral considerations are the marks of a paper tiger; and the sight of a paper tiger incites him to a most reckless ferocity. Never before has there been such a disdain for truth and "the court of world opinion." The intellectual in power seems to understand only the simple language of divisions, warships, bombers, and missiles. He has a most sensitive nose for iron determination. Who would have dreamed fifty years ago that intellectuals ready to give their lives for the oppressed would make an article of faith of cynicism and the big lie? Who would have thought that power would corrupt the idealistic intellectual more than it does any other type of humanity?

The age of the intellectuals is full of surprises and paradoxes. One would have thought, for instance, that in societies dominated by intellectuals the atmosphere would be ideal for the performance of poets, writers, and artists. What we find instead is that a ruling intellectual hierarchy tends to hamper or even stifle the creative individual. The reason for this paradox is that when intellectuals come to power it is as a rule the meagerly endowed among them who rule the roost. The genuinely creative person seems to lack the temperament requisite for the seizure, exercise, and, above all, the retention of power. If Hitler had had the talents of a great painter or architect, if Lenin and Stalin had had the making of great theoreticians, if Napoleon and Mussolini had had it in them to become great poets or philosophers, they might not have developed an unappeasable hunger for power. Now, one of the chief proclivities of people who hunger for literary or artistic greatness but lack talents is to interfere with the creativeness of others. They derive an exquisite satisfaction from imposing their taste and style on the gifted and the brilliant. Throughout most of history the creative intellectual was at his best in societies dominated not by "men

81

of words" but by men of action who were culturally literate. In Florence of the Renaissance, Cosimo the Elder, a banker who dreamed of having God the Father on his books as a debtor, reverenced talent the way the pious reverence saints. Though he was first in the state, and unequaled in fortune and prestige, he played the humble disciple to scholars, poets and artists.

And how do the common people fare in societies possessed by intellectuals?

It is well to remember that all through history the masses have found the intellectual a most formidable taskmaster. In the past, rule by intellectuals went hand in hand with the subjection or even the enslavement of those who do the world's work. In India and China where scholarly Brahmins and Mandarins were at the top for millennia the lot of the masses was oppression, famine, and grinding poverty. In no other societies have the weak been treated so mercilessly. In ancient Greece an aristocracy of intellectuals, unequaled in body and mind, had its foot on the neck of a large population of slaves. Even in Palestine, where after the return from Babylonian exile the scribes and their successors, the Pharisees, were in power, the common people were considered outcasts unfit even for piety. During the Middle Ages a hierarchy of clerks left the common people to sink into serfdom and superstitious darkness.

One cannot escape the impression that the intellectual's most fundamental incompatibility is with the masses. In every age since the invention of writing he has given words to his loathing of the common man. Yet, knowing all this, we were not prepared for the fate that has befallen the masses in the present age of the intellectuals. A ruling intelligentsia, whether in Europe, Asia or Africa, treats the masses as raw material to be experimented on, processed, and wasted at will. Charles Péguy saw it long ago, before the First World War. The intellectuals, he said, dealt with people the way a manufacturer deals with wares; they were *capitalists of people.* Yet the ruling intellectuals see themselves as champions and spokesmen of the people, and call their societies "people's democracies."

When the intellectuals come to power they develop a profound mistrust of mankind. They do not trust each other, but their deepest mistrust is of the common people. Tell a Russian, Chinese, or Cuban commissar that the masses, if left to themselves, would perform well, and he will laugh to your face. He knows that the masses are incurably lazy, stupid and dishonest. You have to watch them all the time, breathe down their necks, push them, and crack the whip if you want to get anything done. The ratio between supervisory and producing personnel is always highest where the intellectuals are in power. In a Communist country it takes half the population to supervise the other half.

The intellectual does not believe in high wages. Affluence, he thinks, corrupts the people. He wants them to work not for filthy money but for a holy cause, for the fatherland, for glory, honor, the future. He wants to ennoble them by making them work for words. The ability to induce people to work for words can, of course, be of vital importance to poor countries trying to get ahead. But enthusiasm is perishable and cannot serve for the long haul. Sooner or later, the working people in societies ruled by intellectuals refuse to perform. They labor-fake, act dumb, and pilfer the cargo the moment the intellectual turns his back. They cannot be frightened with prison since in these societies the difference between life outside and inside prison is one of degree rather than of kind.

So you have to introduce the death penalty for economic offenses, and you have to build high wire fences and brick walls to keep the masses from running away.

Closely allied to the intellectual's attitude toward the masses is his incompatibility with America. With rare exceptions, foreign intellectuals, even when their interests incline them toward us, cannot really stomach America. In France some years ago, the French writer François Mauriac found himself at a lunch table with Cardinal Spellman. He tells us that all the time he was conscious of a feeling of revulsion. "Most probably," he says, "I would have felt closer to the Dalai Lama." This from a very Catholic French intellectual about an American cardinal. British intellectuals have said they felt more at home in France, Germany, Russia, and even in India than in English-speaking America.

Wherever American influence penetrates it rouses the fear and the hostility of the intellectuals. What is there in American influence that so offends and frightens the foreign intellectual? What happens when a country begins to become Americanized? We have been told so often that America has a business civilization that you would expect American influence to manifest itself first in its effect on foreign businessmen. We find instead that the Americanization of a country means, above all, the de-proletarianization of its working class—the stiffening of the workingman's backbone, and the sharpening of his appetites. He not only begins to believe that he is as good as anyone else but wants to live and look like anyone else. In other words, the Americanization of a country amounts to giving it a classless aspect, a sameness that suggests equality. It is this that the foreign intellectual fears and resents. He feels the loss of the aristocratic climate as a private hurt. It is a drab, uninspiring world where every mother's son thinks himself as good as anyone else, and the capacity for reverence and worship becomes atrophied. This to the intellectual is a truly "godless" world, and this the "vulgarity" and the "debasement" against which he rails.

Nothing so offends the doctrinaire intellectual as our ability to achieve the momentous in a matter-of-fact way, unblessed by words. Think of it: our unprecedented productive capacity, our affluence, our freedom and equality are not the end product of a sublime ideology, an absolute truth, or a Promethean struggle. The skyscrapers, the huge factories, dams, powerhouses, docks, railroads, highways, airports, parks, farms stem mostly from the utterly trivial motivation of profit. In the eyes of the foreign intellectual, American achievements are illegitimate, uninstructive and uninspiring. An Indian intellectual protested that America has nothing to teach the world because all her achievements came about by chance.

Equally galling is the fact that until now America has run its complex economy and governmental machinery without the aid of the typical intellectual, and wherever American influence penetrates, the services of the intellectual somehow cease to be indispensable. When an American consulting firm was brought in to straighten out the affairs of a South American company, the first thing it did was fire two-thirds of the pencil pushers, most of whom were university graduates who would rather starve than perform manual labor.

The intellectual's hostility toward America is of long standing. Heine spoke of this country as "the prison of freedom" and saw in our equality a tyranny more stifling than any despotism. Carlyle and a whole tribe of nineteenth-century British intellectuals were appalled by our commonness and alarmed by our materialism. Renan saw the end product of our democracy as "a degenerate populace having no other aim than to indulge the ignoble appetites of the vulgar."* Freud protested: "I do not hate America, I regret it. I regret that Columbus discovered it." In his "Reflections on America" Jacques Maritain tells in vivid words how the foreign intellectuals, out of their fear and hatred of the common man, have been telling each other that the common man's continent is "a great death continent populated only with machines and walking corpses," a world "only intent on sucking all the vitality and the creative instinct of the universe in order to foster with them the levelling power of dead matter and a swarm of automatic ghouls."

Thus it seems that the protagonists of our present age are not America and Russia, or America and China, or Russia and China, but America and the intellectuals. Though the indications are that America will somehow man-

---

* Saul Bellow echoed Renan when he said that affluence has "left us without a system of values" and made of America "a pig heaven."

age to come to terms with governments by intellectuals in Europe, the prospects are not promising for a modus vivendi with dominant intellectuals in Asia, Africa, and Latin America. A letter recently received from an American diplomat serving in Asia says: "I am always surprised at the amount of raw, venomous hatred for the U.S. that is displayed by everyone with more than six years of education in this part of the world. Strangely, the poor and illiterate masses remain well disposed toward the U.S., but that will certainly disappear with the next generation. . . . By recognizing as a constant factor the hostility of the underdeveloped intellectuals, we could avoid the costly effort involved in trying to win world public opinion, and cold-bloodedly realize what they already know—that we are by our basic nature and destiny a subversive force in these societies, and that our own security lies in the transfer of power to the masses and to real mass leaders, not elite class leaders."

Time seems to be working for the intellectuals. With the spread of automation the intellectuals will be everywhere on top, and the common people unneeded and unwanted. In Dostoyevsky's *The Possessed* a brash intellectual shoots his mouth off on the subject: "For my part, if I didn't know what to do with nine-tenths of mankind, I'd take them and blow them up into the air instead of putting them in paradise. I'd leave only a handful of educated people who would live happily ever afterward on scientific principles." I am quite certain that nothing of this sort is going to happen to us. Still, the question remains: How can the common people safeguard themselves against tyranny by an intellectocracy? Strangely enough, the answer, though not easy, is relatively simple. Just as tyranny by an aristocracy or a plutocracy can be most effectively checked by turning everyone into an aristocrat or a capitalist, so tyranny by an intellectocracy can be neutralized by turning everyone into an intellectual. This, of course, means society as a university, with a Berkeley-style "Free Speech Movement" acting as a formidable opposition against tyranny from any quarter.

Since the central concern of the Great Society must be the realization and cultivation of its human resources, it might have to turn itself into a school even if there were no need for a safeguard against any sort of tyranny. But as we try to visualize society as a school—a country divided into hundreds of thousands of small school districts, each charged with the realization of its natural and human resources—we find the pleasant surprise that what we have would be less society as a school than society as a playground. A wholly automated economy would demand only a token effort from the individual and give him back the child's freedom to play. The relatively small number of people in each school district, with their various interests and pursuits, would have the time and the inclination to know each other, learn from and teach each other, compete with and spur each other. There would be no dividing line between learning and living. All that schoolmasters can teach in a schoolroom is as nothing when compared with what we cannot help teaching each other on a playground. "Man," said Walter Bagehot, "made the school; God the playground."

5   *The Return of Nature*

ALL THROUGH ADULT LIFE I had a feeling of
revulsion when told how nature aids and
guides us, how like a stern mother she nudges
and pushes man to fulfill her wise designs. As
a migratory worker from the age of eighteen
I knew nature as ill-disposed and inhospitable.
If I stretched on the ground to rest, nature
pushed its hard knuckles into my sides, and
sent bugs, burs, and foxtails to make me get
up and be gone. As a placer miner I had to
run the gantlet of buckbrush, manzanita, and
poison oak when I left the road to find my way
to a creek. Direct contact with nature almost
always meant scratches, bites, torn clothes, and

grime that ate its way into every pore of the body. To make life bearable I had to inter-pose a protective layer between myself and nature. On the paved road, even when miles from anywhere, I felt at home. I had a sense of kinship with the winding, endless road that cares not where it goes and what its load.

Almost all the books I read spoke worship-fully of nature. Nature was pure, innocent, serene, health-giving, bountiful, the fountain-head of elevated thoughts and noble feelings. It seemed that every writer was a "nature boy." I assumed that these people had no share in the world's work, and did not know nature at close quarters. It also seemed to me that they had a grievance. For coupled with their admiration of nature was a distaste for man and man's work. Man was a violator, a defiler and deformer.

The truth about nature I found in the news-papers, in the almost daily reports of floods, tornados, blizzards, hurricanes, typhoons, hailstorms, sandstorms, earthquakes, ava-lanches, eruptions, inundations, pests, plagues, and famines. Sometimes when reading about nature's terrible visitations and her massacre of the innocents it seemed to me that we are surrounded by devouring, pitiless forces, that the earth was full of anger, the sky dark with wrath, and that man had built the city as a refuge from a hostile, nonhuman cosmos. I realized that the contest between man and nature has been the central drama of the universe.

Man became what he is not with the aid, but in spite, of nature. Humanization meant breaking away from nature, getting out from underneath the iron necessities which dominate nature. By the same token, dehumanization means the reclamation of man by nature. It means the return of nature. It is significant that humanization had its start in the fact that man was an unfinished, defective animal. Nature dealt niggardly with him from the beginning. It brought him forth naked and helpless, without inborn skills, and without specialized organs to serve him as weapons and tools. Unlike other animals, man was not a born technician with a built-in tool kit. Small wonder that for millennia man worshiped animals, nature's more favored children. Yet this misbegotten creature has made himself lord of the globe. He has evolved fabulous substitutes for the instincts and the specialized organs that he lacked, and rather than adjust himself to the world he has changed the world to fit him. This, surely, is the supreme miracle. If history is to have meaning it must be the history of humanization, of man's tortuous ascent through the ages, of his ceaseless effort to break away from the rest of creation and become an order apart.

Man became human by finishing himself. Yet his humanness is never finished and final. Man is not only an unfinished animal; he is an unfinished man. His human uniqueness is something he had to achieve and preserve. Nature is always around and within us, ready to reclaim us and sweep away all that man has wrought and achieved. Man's chief goal in life is still to become and stay human, and defend his achievements against the encroachment of nature. Nature is in almost complete possession of us when we are born. The child has to be brought up and made human. And no sooner is this accomplished than comes a crisis, the transition from childhood to manhood, in which nature reasserts itself. The humanness of the adolescent is a precarious thing. He has to be reborn to manhood and be rehumanized. Indeed, every drastic change from one way of life to another constitutes a strain which may crack the uppermost layers of the mind, and lay bare the less human layers. Hence a time of drastic change, even when the change is a leap forward, is a time of barbarization. Each generation has to humanize itself.

The contest with nature has the refined trickery we have come to associate with totalitarian wars. There are fifth columns, subversion, and a constant probing for soft spots. Just as man uses the forces of nature to subdue nature, so does nature use men to dehumanize their fellow men; and it is in the city that nature's fifth column finds its most fertile ground. The birth of the city was a crucial step in man's separation from nature. The city cut man off not only from the nonhuman cosmos but also from clans, tribes, and other primitive modes of organization. A self-governing city populated by more or less autonomous individuals has been the cradle of freedom, art, literature, science, and technology. But the city that has been a citadel against the nature around us cannot defend us against the nature within us, in our lusts and fears, and in the subconscious cellars of our minds. It is in the city that man's lusts and fears have free play, and dehumanization spreads like the plague. The lust for power in

97

particular has shown itself to be antihuman. We savor power not when we move mountains and tell rivers whither to flow but when we can turn men into objects, robots, puppets, automata, or veritable animals. Power is power to dehumanize, and it is in the city that this lust finds the human material to work on. It is easier to dehumanize man in the mass than any individual man. Thus the city has been the breeding ground of all movements and developments that tend to press man back into the matrix of nature from which he has risen.

A fateful feature of the war with nature is its circularity. Victory and defeat run into each other. Just when man seems to be within reach of his ultimate goal he is likely to find himself caught in a trap. Everywhere there are booby traps and pitfalls, and nature strikes back from unexpected quarters. A most recent example is the splitting of the atom. Man cracked nature's strongbox only to discover that he had cracked Pandora's box of ills and woes and evil spirits, and let loose the poisonous mushroom cloud of total annihilation.

One thinks of the fantastic spectacle of the nineteenth century when the Industrial Revolution seemed to make man's dream of total victory over nature come true, and the prospect of a man-made world blanketing the whole of the globe seemed within reach. The fateful fact that man was not inventive enough to automate his second creation, that his machines were half-machines lacking the gears and filaments of thought and will, set in motion a process of mass dehumanization that turned the machine age into a nightmare. Human beings had to be used as a stopgap for inventiveness. Men, women, and children were coupled with iron and steam. The machines were consuming human beings as fast as coal. It was as if nature had infiltrated the metal of the machines and subverted the man-made world. Factories, mass armies, and mass movements combined to strip people of their human uniqueness and transmute them into a homogeneous, malleable mass. Lenin, the leader of a mass movement, recognized that the "hard school" of the factory was readying people for a totalitarian dictatorship. The mass armies trained people to obedience and mass action. At the same time, Lenin's revolution saw as its main task the conversion of peasants into factory workers and soldiers. Thus industrialists, generals, and revolutionaries worked hand in hand. And not they alone. Carlyle's glorification of brute force,

Gobineau's race theories, Marx's economic determinism and his theory of the class struggle, Darwin's and Pavlov's zoological sociology, the dark forces of Wagner's music, Nietzsche's cult of the superman, and Freud's emphasis on the less human components of man's soul were all part of a blind striving to reintegrate man with nature. The deliberate dehumanization practiced by Stalin and Hitler was an intensification and acceleration of something that had been going on for decades. There is hardly an enormity committed in the twentieth century that was not foreshadowed and even advocated by some noble "man of words" in the nineteenth. Even such clearcut opposites as the fascination with science and the romantic back-to-nature movements were actually pulling in the same direction—helping to equate man with nature, and cooperating in the dehumanization of man. They who leaped ahead and they who plunged backward arrived simultaneously at the gates of the twentieth-century annihilation camps.

One of the strangest features of man's war with nature is its undeclaredness. The men who are in the forefront of the battle are as a rule unaware that they are fighting a war. They are usually animated by a hunger for profit or for spectacular action. I have not come across a clarion call to mankind to abandon war between brothers and mobilize all its energies in a titanic struggle with the nonhuman universe. You can count on the fingers of one hand unequivocal expressions of the eternal enmity between man and nature. I can think only of Hardy's "Man begins where nature ends; nature and man can never be friends." Thoreau, who sided with nature, recognized that "you cannot have a deep sympathy with both man and nature," and admitted, "I love nature because she is not man but a retreat from him." Toward the end of his life Thomas Huxley realized that man's ascent was something different from his descent. In his Romanes lecture, in 1893, he warned: "Let us understand once for all that the ethical progress of societies depends not on imitating the cosmic process, still less in running away from it, but in combatting it."

There is an echo of man's first blows against nature in some myths. The Babylonian God Marduk slayed the dragon Tiamath and created arable land of her carcass. Prometheus stole fire from the gods and gave it to man to compensate him for the meagerness of his physical endowments. Yet, on the whole, the impression conveyed by mythologies is of a close relationship between man and nature in which nature always has the upper hand and must be supplicated and propitiated. There is a Darwinian motif in the totemic assumption of a kinship between man and other forms of life. The whole structure of magic is founded on an identity between human nature and nature. Both the scientist and the savage postulate the oneness of man and nature. The difference between them is that the savage tries to influence nature by means which have proved their efficacy in influencing human nature, while the scientist wants to deal with human nature the way he deals with matter and other forms of life. The scientist reads the equation *human nature = nature* from left to right, while the savage reads it from right to left. Yet it is worth noting that Darwin, too, read the equation from right to left when he read cutthroat capitalist competition into the economy of nature.

In this as in other fields the uniqueness of the ancient Hebrews is startlingly striking. They were the first to enunciate a clear-cut separation between man and nature. Though monotheism was born of tribal pride—the desire to be the one and only people of a one and only God—it brought with it a downgrading of nature. The one and only God created both nature and man yet made man in His own image and appointed him His viceroy on earth. Jehovah's injunction to man (Genesis, Chapter 1) is unequivocal: Be fruitful and multiply and subdue the earth. Nature lost its divine attributes. Sun, stars, sky, earth, mountains, rivers, plants, and animals were no longer the seat of mysterious powers and the arbiters of man's fate. Though man had to wrestle with the earth for his bread, he was the masterful male ADAM, and the earth, ADAMA, a female to be beaten into submission. The writers of the Old Testament picked as the father of the race not Esau, a man of nature, whose garments, like those of Thoreau's ideal man, smelled of grassy fields and flowery meadows, but his twin Jacob, who was all too human in his anxieties and cunning scheming, and who preferred the inside of a tent to the great outdoors, and the smell of lentil soup to the smell of trees and fields.

It is true that the downgrading of nature did not prompt the ancient Hebrews to become mighty tamers of nature. Still, their endurance as a weak minority through centuries of persecution constitutes a grand defiance of nature, a putting to naught of the law of survival of the strong which rules the rest of life. Moreover, the mighty Jehovah did play a role in the rise of the scientific and technological civilization of the modern Occident. It is hard for us to realize how god-conscious were the scientists and technologists active at the birth of the modern Occident. Jehovah was to them the supreme mathematician and technician who had created the world and set it going. To unravel the mysteries of nature was to decipher God's text and rethink His thoughts. When Kepler formulated the laws of planetary motion he boasted that God had to wait six thousand years for His first reader. These early scientists and technicians felt close to God; they stood in awe of Him yet felt as if they were of His school, and whether they knew it or not aspired to be like Him. Perhaps one of the reasons that other civilizations, with all their ingenuity and skill, did not develop a machine age is that they had no God who was an all-powerful engineer whom they could imitate and vie with.

The first great assault upon nature took place in the Neolithic Age when there was as yet no writing; thus it remained unrecorded and unsung. Yet it is legitimate to wonder whether the presence of scribes would have mattered one way or another—whether the "men of words" would have been aware of the import of that which was happening before their eyes, let alone moved enough to declaim and sing. For when the second great assault came in the nineteenth century the "men of words" were not in the fight, and, indeed, a great many of them sided with nature against man. It was precisely at the moment when the Industrial Revolution forged the weapons for a total victory over nature that scientists, poets, philosophers, and historians, seized with a mysterious impulse, began to proclaim with one voice the littleness of man and his powerlessness to shape his fate. Man, declared Huxley in 1860, "strives in vain to break through the ties which hold him to matter and the lower forms of life." Instead of being in the vanguard of the Promethean struggle we find the most gifted members of the species on the sidelines jeering at the clamorous multitude that set out to tame and straddle God's creation.

The intellectuals entered the nineteenth century flushed with the conviction that they were the new makers of history. Had not their words set in motion the earthshaking events of the French Revolution? Coleridge boasted that the most important changes in the world had their origin not in the cabinets of statesmen or the insights of businessmen but "in the closets and lonely walks of theorists." Heine was more blatant: "Mark this ye proud men of action; ye are nothing but unconscious instruments of men of thought who, often in the humblest seclusion, have appointed you to your inevitable tasks." Few of the educated knew in the first decades of the nineteenth century that they had an Industrial Revolution on their hands. Everywhere the intellectuals were strutting, posturing, and declaiming, each fancying himself a man of destiny. Then one morning they woke up to discover that power had fallen into the hands of their middle-class relatives, their lowbrow brothers, uncles, in-laws, who had not only taken possession of everything they could lay their hands on, but aspired to impose their values and tastes upon the whole society. The revulsion from a middle-class society that came to dominate the nineteenth century alienated the intellectuals from the machine age. Writers, poets, artists, philosophers, and scholars poured their scorn on the money-grubbing, mean-spirited, sweating, pushing, hard-working philistines who dared vie with God. "The steam engine," cried Baudelaire, "is a negation of God." Flaubert described his joy at the sight of weeds overrunning abandoned buildings, "this embrace of nature coming swiftly to bury the work of man the moment that his hand is no longer there to defend it." One also wonders how much the refusal to countenance history made by a despised middle class contributed to the tendency of the learned during the nineteenth century to downgrade man as a maker of history.

The cold war between the intellectuals and the middle class that started more than a century ago has been gathering force in the twentieth century, and the intellectuals seem to be coming out on top. In many parts of the world the intellectual is just now at the center of the stage as ruler, legislator, policeman, military leader, and large-scale industrialist. One of the greatest surprises of the twentieth century was sprung by the educated when they came to power. Gandhi once said that what worried him most was "the hardness of heart of the educated," and it staggers the mind that education rather than educating the heart often makes it more savage. We have discovered that nature prefers to lodge its fifth column in the minds and hearts of the educated. We have yet to assimilate the fact that it took "a nation of philosophers" to produce Hitler and Nazism, and that in Stalin's Russia professors, writers, artists, and scientists were a pampered and petted aristocracy. These privileged intellectuals did not let out a peep against one of the most brutal tyrannies the world has seen. The Stalin cult was the work of intellectuals.*

It is remarkable how worshipful of the machine intellectuals become when the economy of a country is in their keeping, and how naturally they take to treating human beings as a cheap, all-purpose raw material. They have processed human flesh and bone into steel mills, dams, powerhouses, etc., and it was all done in the name of a noble ideal. It needs

---

* Stalin also liquidated intellectuals. The fact that when intellectuals hang together and attain power they often end up by hanging each other underlines the unconditioned savagery of "the bloody-minded professors."

an effort to realize that the twentieth century is the century of the idealist. No other century has seen so vast an expulsion of practical people from the seats of power and their replacement by idealists. In no other century has there been so powerful an attempt to realize ideals, dreams, and visions. The unprecedented dehumanization our century has seen was conceived and engineered by idealists.

Societies ruled by intellectuals tend to approach menageries: the fences and walls which usually enclose them are there not to keep anything out but to keep the animals from running away. The return of nature in these societies manifests itself not only in the attitude of the rulers toward the people, but in the attitude of the ruled toward the government. In a Communist country, for instance, people tend to view the government as a force of nature, and the misfortunes that overtake them as natural calamities. You do not protest or conspire against a natural catastrophe, nor do you feel humiliated when struck down by a natural force. You do not feel humiliated when the ocean spits on you, or the wind forces you to your knees. To outsiders, too, there is something terrifyingly unhuman about these societies. Every child is aware of Russia's and China's unhuman strength, while it needs an exceptional acuteness, a sixth sense almost, to have anything like a realistic grasp of America's capabilities.

Why should power corrupt the intellectual more than it does other types of humanity? One of the reasons is to be found in the assumption that education readies a person for the task of reforming and reshaping humanity —that it equips him to act as an engineer of souls and a manufacturer of desirable human attributes. Hence when power gives him the freedom to act, the intellectual will be inclined to deal with humanity as with material that can be molded and processed. He will arrange things so that he will not be thwarted by the unpredictability and intractability of human nature. The antihumanity of the intellectual in power is not a function of his inhumanity. An elite of intellectuals is more vowed to the service of mankind or of a nation than any other elite. But a savior who wants to turn men into angels will be as much a hater of human nature as a monster who wants to turn them into slaves and animals. Man must be dehumanized, must be turned into an object, before he can be processed into something wholly different from what he is. It is a para-

dox that the idealistic reformer has a me-
chanical, lifeless conception of man's being.
He sees man as something that can be taken
apart and put together, and the renovation of
the individual and of society as a process of
manufacturing. Robert Owen used a manufacturer's vocabulary to describe his intended
reforms not mainly because he was a manufacturer but because he was a reformer. He
spoke of his new social order as "the new machinery" which "will facilitate the larger production of happiness."

Another source of the intellectual's corruption by power is that no matter how
powerful he becomes he continues to utilize
the devices of the weak. It is curious how
even at the height of their power Hitler,
Stalin, Mao, and others tended to speak and
act as if they were the leaders of "a company
of poor men," of an oppressed tribe or a
persecuted minority. Absolute faith and mon-
olithic unity that enable the weak to survive
are unequaled instruments of coercion in the
hands of the powerful.

Finally, intellectuals in power are chronically afraid, and herein lies one more cause of
their corruption by power. For the intellectual
cannot admit to himself what it is that he is

afraid of. When we are aware of the cause of our fear we can be afraid of only one thing, but when we cannot face the truth the fear becomes general. An elite of intellectuals is afraid chiefly of its own people and cannot admit it, hence the fear of the whole world; and when power is mated with a great fear it becomes virulent.

As we have seen, the war with nature proceeds both around and within us, yet we have no precise knowledge how the happenings on one front affect the other. Up to now, an increased command over nature around us did not automatically reinforce our humanness. On the contrary, in many parts of the world the taming of nature by rapid industrialization gave rise to a greater or lesser degree of social barbarization. Some thoughtful persons have questioned the wisdom of seeking further command over nature until means have been devised to prevent the misuse of the enormous power we already have in our hands. Nevertheless, the overcoming of nature, so crucial in the ascent of man, can be a most effective agency of humanization in the decades ahead—if for no other reason than that it may divert aggressive impulses and wild energies from social strife. We are told that a decade from now 60 percent of the people in this country will be eighteen and under. The Negro population is already more than half juvenile, and the same is true of the populations of Latin America, Asia, and Africa. The presence of a global population of juveniles spells trouble for everybody. No country is a good country for its juveniles, and even in normal times every society is in the grip of a crisis when a new generation passes from boyhood to manhood. The enemy is within the gates. The trouble with the juvenile is not that he is not as yet a man but that he is no longer a child. He has lost the child's capacity for wonder and for total absorption in whatever it does, and its hunger to master skills. The juvenile's self-consciousness robs him of genuineness, while his penchant for self-dramatization prompts him to extremist poses and gestures. In his restless groping for an identity he will join any mass movement and plunge into any form of spectacular action. His humanness is a precarious thing, easily sloughed off. Both the Bolsheviks and the Fascists made use of juveniles to do the dirty work of killing.

My feeling is that the humanization of bil-

lions of adolescents would be greatly facili-
tated by a concerted undertaking to master
and domesticate the whole of the globe. One
would like to see mankind spend the balance
of the century in a total effort to clean up
and groom the surface of the globe—wipe
out the jungles, turn deserts and swamps into
arable land, terrace barren mountains, regulate rivers, eradicate all pests, control the
weather, and make the whole land mass a fit
habitation for man. The globe should be our
and not nature's home, and we no longer nature's guests. A hundred years ago Alfred Rus-
sel Wallace envisioned the time "When man's
selection shall have supplanted natural selection; when the ocean would be the only domain in which that power can be exerted
which for countless cycles of ages ruled supreme over all the earth." So, too, did the
prophet Isaiah envision total domestication at
the end of time when the wolf and the lamb,
the leopard and the kid, the lion and the calf,
the bear and the cow shall lie down together,
and a little child shall lead them.

There is a phase of the war with nature
which is little noticed but has always impressed
me. To me there is an aura of grandeur about

the dull routine of maintenance: I see it as a
defiance of the teeth of time. It is easier to
build than to maintain. Even a lethargic or
debilitated population can be galvanized for a
while to achieve something impressive, but
the energy which goes into maintaining things
in good repair day in, day out is the energy
of true vigor. When at the end of the last war
several Western European countries lay in
ruins, one could probably have predicted
which of them would recover first by looking
up their records of maintenance. So, too, in
present-day Africa where some thirty new
nations have come into existence, one might
guess which of them is likely to be here fifty
years from now by looking for rudiments of
maintenance.

From talking with foreign-born longshoremen and ships' crews I gained the impression that the capacity for maintenance is
a peculiarity of Western Europe, the Scandi-
navian countries, the Anglo-Saxon world,
and Japan. The reports of travelers confirm
this impression. Lord Kinross, while traveling
in Turkey, was struck that though the Turks
made excellent mechanics they had no talent
for maintenance; "indeed, until lately no word
for maintenance existed in the Turkish lan-

guage." Mr. André Siegfried sees the process of maintenance as "something which belongs essentially to the Westerner" and thinks "it is here that we must look for his distinct characteristic."

It is strange that in Asia, where civilization had its birth, the separation from nature and the ability to hold it at bay should be much less pronounced than in the younger civilization of the Occident. In Asia, Africa, and Latin America the man-made world seems precariously stretched over the writhing body of nature. At the edge of every cultivated field, and around every human habitation, nature lies in wait ready to move in and repossess what man has wrested from its grasp. You see trees cracking walls, heaving blocks of stone from their sockets, and reclaiming once mighty cities. In Australia nature reclaimed the dog from its human domesticator and almost reclaimed man himself. One has the feeling that the true awakening and modernization of a backward country is hardly conceivable without the evolvement of the capacity for maintenance.

There is the story about Georges Clemenceau that when he traveled around the world in 1921 he came to New Delhi and was taken to see the huge Baker-Lutyen office buildings which were just then completed. He stood gazing at the buildings for a long time without uttering a word. Finally, the British officer who was with him asked what he thought of them. "I was thinking," said Clemenceau, "what ruins these will make!" As so often with Clemenceau, his chance remark threw a searching light on the human situation. Standing at the heart of Asia, Clemenceau felt himself primarily an Occidental and saw the British Empire as Occidental rather than British. He also knew that the days of the Occident in Asia were numbered, and that, once the Occident withdrew its hand, the dragon of Asia would move in and sink its yellowed teeth of time into all that the Occident had built and wrought, and gnaw away till naught was left but a skeleton of ruins.

6 — *Some Thoughts on the Present*

It is remarkable that after a century of incessant change the paths of change have not become smooth and easy. On the contrary, our world seems to be getting less and less suitable for people who undergo change. Never before has the passage from boyhood to manhood been so painful and so beset with explosions. The passage from backwardness to modernity which in the nineteenth century seemed a natural process is now straining a large part of the world to the breaking point. The hoped-for changes from poverty to affluence, from subjection to freedom, from work to leisure do not enhance social stability but threaten social dissolution. However noble the intentions and whole-hearted the efforts of those who initiate change, the results are often the opposite of that which was reasonable to expect. Social chemistry has gone awry: no matter what ingredients are placed in the retort, the end product is more often than not an explosive.

If one were to pick the chief trait which characterizes the temper of our time it would be impatience. Tomorrow has become a dirty word. The future is now, and hope has turned into desire. The adolescent cannot see why he should wait to become a man before he has a say in the ordering of domestic and foreign affairs. The backward, also, panting to catch up tomorrow with our yesterdays, want to act as pathfinders in the van of mankind. Everywhere you look you see countries leaping. There is no time to grow. New countries want to bloom and bear fruit even as they sprout, and many have decked themselves out with artificial flowers and fruit.

Everywhere there is a greed for pride. Pride is the only currency that will buy souls. In the backward countries an undertaking will make headway only if it generates pride. These countries find it easier to induce a readiness to fight and die than a readiness to work, easier to attempt the impossible than the possible, easier to build dams and steel mills than raise wheat, easier to start at the end and work backward than begin at the beginning. Never has giving been so urgent and the act of giving so difficult. To preserve your pride you must vilify those who help you. You accuse them of practicing the colonialism of giving. Rudeness has become a substitute for power, for faith, and for achievement.

Amidst the leaping, running, and shouting no one can tell whether the momentous events of our time are real and not merely the echo of words. How real are the new nations? Is the Occident really in decline? And who can tell with certitude whether the world is being Communized or Americanized?

So evanescent are world situations that we cannot suit our actions to facts. Never has the present been so perishable: things which happened yesterday are ancient history. The better part of statesmanship might be to know clearly and precisely what not to do, and leave action to the improvisation of chance. It might be wise to wait for our enemies to defeat themselves, and heed Bacon's advice to treat friends as if they might one day become our enemies, and enemies as if they might one day become our friends.

The decline of the Occident has been proclaimed on housetops for over half a century. Knowledgeable people are still telling us that Europe is finished, America rotten to the core, and that the future is in Russia, China, India, Africa, and even in Latin America. We are urged to learn the meaning of life from these bearers of the future. Yet it is becoming evident that if there is going to be anywhere a genuine growth of individual freedom and human dignity it will be from cuttings taken from the Occident. Even the Communist parties of the Occident are discovering that their historical role is not to change the Occident's way of life but to put a brake on the dehumanizing juggernaut of the Communist apparatus in Russia and China.

The fact is that the awakening of Asia and Africa has turned the Occident into a mystery. When we see to what ugly stratagems the new countries have to resort in order to make their people do the things which we consider natural and matter-of-fact we begin to realize how unprecedented the Occident is with its spontaneous enterprise and orderliness, and its elementary decencies. The mystery of our time is not the enigmatic Orient but the fantastic Occident.

The Occident is at present without fervent faith and hope. There is no overwhelming undertaking in sight that might set minds and hearts on fire. There is no singular happiness and no excessive suffering. We have already discounted every possible invention, and reduced momentous tasks to sheer routine. Though we are aware of deadly dangers ahead of us, our fears have not affected our rhythm of life. The Occident continues to function well at room temperature.

Now, there are those who maintain that lack of a strong faith must in the long run prove fatal to a society, and that the most decisive changes in history are those which involve a weakening or intensification of belief. Whether this be true or not it should be clear that a weakening of faith can be due as much to a gain in power, skill, and experience as to a loss of vigor and drive. Where there is the necessary skill and equipment to move mountains there is no need for the faith that moves mountains. Intensification of belief is not necessarily a symptom of vigor, nor does a fading of belief spell decline. The strong, unless they are infected with a pathological fear, cannot generate and sustain a strong faith. Nowhere in the Occident is there at present a faith comparable to that which is being generated in the meek, backward masses of Russia and China. The Occident has skill, efficiency, orderliness, and a phenomenal readiness to work. It would be suicidal for the Occident to rely on a concocted new faith in a contest with totalitarian countries. We can prevail only by doing more and better what we know how to do well. Those in the Occident who wring their hands and pray for a new faith are sowing the wind.

Free men are aware of the imperfection inherent in human affairs, and they are willing to fight and die for that which is not perfect. They know that basic human problems can have no final solutions, that our freedom, justice, equality, etc. are far from absolute, and that the good life is compounded of half measures, compromises, lesser evils, and gropings toward the perfect. The rejection of approximations and the insistence on absolutes are the manifestation of a nihilism that loathes freedom, tolerance, and equity.

The present Americanization of the world is an unprecedented phenomenon. The penetration of a foreign influence has almost always depended on the hospitableness of the educated and the well-to-do. Yet the world-wide diffusion of American habits, fashions, and ways is proceeding in the teeth of the shrill opposition of the intellectuals and the hostility of the better people. The only analogy which comes to mind is the early spread of Christianity, with the difference that Americanization is not being pushed by apostles and missionaries but like a chemical reagent penetrates of its own accord and instantly combines with the common people and the young. "The American way of life," says a British observer, "has become the religion of the masses in five continents."*

Ironically, at a time when the world is being Americanized the American intellectual seems to be seceding from America. Here in the San Francisco Bay area, the dramatic change in the intellectual's attitude toward America has the earmarks of a historical turning point. The first impression is that the American intellectual is being Europeanized, and one is tempted to see a connection between influ-

* David Marquand in the Manchester *Guardian Weekly,* March 17, 1960.

encing and being influenced: that by influencing the world America unavoidably opens itself up to foreign influences; and in this case, as so often before, the intellectual is the carrier of the foreign influence. Actually, the intellectual's revulsion from contemporary America has little to do with the penetration of a foreign influence but is the result of a recent change in the tilt of the social landscape.

The nature of a society is largely determined by the direction in which talent and ambition flow—by the tilt of the social landscape. In America, until recently, most of the energy, ability, and ambition found its outlet in business. In *Notes of a Son and Brother* Henry James tells how, as children, he and his brother William were mortified that their father was not a businessman but a philosopher and an author. In a European country like France, where writers and artists rank high in public esteem, boys and girls probably find it humiliating to admit that their father is a mere businessman and not a writer or an artist. In France, said Oscar Wilde, "every bourgeois wants to be an artist." Now, it stands to reason that the central pursuit of a society attracts and swallows individuals who by nature are meant for other careers. In America, until recently, many potential poets and philosophers became businessmen, while in France many potential business tycoons go through life as intellectuals; and the paradox is that these misplaced individuals who do not really belong are often the ones who shape the character and style of the sphere in which they operate. It was not conventional businessmen but misplaced poets and philosophers who set in motion the vast combinations and the train of ceaseless innovation which gave American business its Promethean sweep and drive. To a philosopher who finds himself immersed in a milieu of sheer action, all action will seem of one kind and he will shift easily from one field of activity to another. He will combine factories, mines, railroads, oil wells, etc. the way a philosopher collates and generalizes ideas. In France, where the misplaced individuals are chiefly among the intellectuals, the tone and the pace of the intellectual establishment are generated not by authentic intellectuals to whom words and ideas are ends in themselves, the center of existence, but by potential men of action, potential organizers and administrators, who find themselves trapped in the

127

mold of intellectuals. To this type of intellectual ideas have validity only as a prelude to
action, and he sees commitment and history
making as vital components of an intellectual
existence.

Now, the important fact is that since Sput-
nik the prestige and material rewards of intellectual pursuits have risen sharply in this country, and the social landscape has begun to tilt
away from business. Right now the career of
a scientist or a professor can be more excit-
ing than that of a businessman, and its material rewards are not to be sneezed at. A recent survey showed that only 20 percent of
undergraduates intend to go into business.
The chances are great, therefore, that at present many individuals with superb talents for
wheeling and dealing and for building industrial empires are pawing their way up the
academic ladder or are throwing their weight
around in literary and artistic circles. This is
a state of affairs not unlike that which prevails
in France, hence the impression that the
American intellectual is being Europeanized.

It goes without saying that a change in the
direction of flow of social energies constitutes
a turning point in the life of a society or a
civilization. If the Reformation figured as

a historical turning point, and marked the birth of the modern Occident, it was largely because it brought about a diversion of energies from sacerdotal to secular channels. We are told that during a twenty-year period in the sixteenth century not a student of the University of Vienna became a priest. In this country, with the opening of the West in the middle of the last century, the sons of New England divines, poets, writers, and scholars went into railroading, mining, and manufacturing, and this diversion of energies from one field to another marked the birth of modern America and also brought to an almost abrupt end the cultural flowering of New England.

There is no telling how soon and to what degree the diversion of talent and ambition from business might make itself felt in a diminution of economic venturesomeness and drive. Nor can we tell whether the inflow of energies into intellectual pursuits will result in an upsurge of cultural creativeness. But it is beyond doubt that the movers and shakers are already at work inside and outside the universities. The civil rights movement and the Vietnam war are ideal vehicles for these would-be makers of history. History making is becoming the malady of our age: the book of history seems to lie open and every two-bit intellectual wants to turn its pages.

The attitude of the intellectual community toward America is shaped not by the creative few but by the many who for one reason or another cannot transmute their dissatisfaction into a creative impulse, and cannot acquire a sense of uniqueness and of growth by developing and expressing their capacities and talents. There is nothing in contemporary America that can cure or alleviate their chronic frustration. They want power, lordship, and opportunities for imposing action. Even if we should banish poverty from the land, lift up the Negro to true equality, withdraw from Vietnam, and give half of the national income as foreign aid, they will still see America as an airconditioned nightmare unfit for them to live in.

When you try to find out what it is in this country that stifles the American intellectual, you make a surprising discovery. It is not the landscape, though he is poignantly aware of its historical meagerness, and it is not the social system, particularly when it is headed by aristocrats like Roosevelt and Kennedy. What he cannot stomach is the mass of the American people—a mindless monstrosity devoid of spiritual, moral, and intellectual capacities. Like the aging Henry Adams, the contemporary American intellectual scans the daily newspapers for evidence of the depravity and perversity of American life, and arms himself with a battery of clippings to fortify his loathing and revulsion. When you listen to him or read what he writes about America you begin to suspect that what the American intellectuals know about the American people is actually what they know about each other: that they project upon America the infighting, mistrust, envy, malice, conformity, meagerness, and staleness of their cliques and sects. Imagine an American writing about America and not mentioning kindness, not mentioning the boundless capacity for working together, not mentioning the unprecedented diffusion of social, political, as well as technological skills, not mentioning the American's ability to do the world's work with a minimum of supervision and leadership, not mentioning the breathtaking potentialities which lurk in the commonest American. Who among the intellectuals would have predicted that a machine politician patronized by the Knowlands would become Chief Justice Earl Warren, that a hack politician endorsed by the Ku Klux

Klan would become Justice Hugo Black, that a bankrupt haberdasher who was given his start by the corrupt Pendergast machine would become President Harry Truman, that a Southern politician would push through the civil rights legislation. The Johnsons, Trumans, Blacks, and Warrens can be met in every walk of life, and they are wholly immersed in American life.

The American intellectual rejects the idea that our ability to do things with little tutelage and leadership is a mark of social vigor. He would gauge the vigor of a society by its ability to produce great leaders. Yet it is precisely an America that in normal times can function well without outstanding leaders that so readily throws up outstanding individuals. When you talk to an American intellectual about common Americans it is as if you were talking about mysterious people living on a mysterious continent.

Yet when all is said about the intellectual's preposterous stance there remains the incontestable fact that his chronic militancy and carping have been a vital factor in the Occident's social progress. The blast of the intellectual's trumpets has not brought down or damaged our political and economic institutions. Napoleon predicted that ink would do to the modern social organization what cannon had done to the feudal system. Actually, in the Occident, ink has acted more as a detergent than an explosive. It is doubtful whether without the activities of the pen-and-ink tribe the lot of the common people would be what it is now.

The events of the past fifty years have sharpened our awareness of the discrepancy between what the intellectual professes while he battles the status quo, and what he practices when he comes to power, and we are wont to search for the features of a commissar in the face of impassioned protest. Actually a metamorphosis of militant intellectual into commissar requires a specific cultural climate and, so far, has taken place mainly outside the Occident. It is easy to underestimate the part played by Russia's and China's past in the evolvement of their present Marxist systems. A century ago Alexander Herzen predicted that Russian Communism would be Russian autocracy turned upside down. In China, where Mandarin intellectuals had the management of affairs in their keeping for centuries, the present dictatorship of an intellectocracy is more a culmination of, than a rupture with, the past.

In Western Europe and the U.S.A., where the tradition of individual freedom has deep roots in both the educated and the uneducated, the intellectuals cannot be self-righteous enough nor the masses submissive enough to duplicate the Russian and the Chinese experience. Thus in the Occident the militant intellectual is a stable type and a typical irritant; and whenever the influence of the Occident becomes strong enough the chronically disaffected intellectual appears on the scene and pits himself against the prevailing dispensation, even when it is a dispensation powered by his fellow intellectuals. We see this illustrated in the present intellectual unrest in Eastern Europe and Russia, and it is beginning to seem that dominant Communist parties have more to fear from a Western infection than the Occident has to fear from Communist subversion.

Stalin's assertion that "no ruling class has managed without its own intelligentsia" applies of course to a totalitarian regime. A society that can afford freedom can also manage without a kept intelligentsia: it is vigorous enough to endure ceaseless harassment by the most articulate and perhaps most gifted segment of the population. Such harassment is the "eternal vigilance" which we are told is the price of liberty. In a free society internal tensions are not the signs of brewing anarchy but the symptoms of vigor—the elements of a self-generating dynamism. Though there is no unequivocal evidence that the intellectual is at his creative best in a wholly free society, it is indubitable that his incorporation in, or close association with, a ruling elite sooner or later results in social and cultural stagnation. The chronic frustration of the intellectual's hunger for power and lordship not only prompts him to side with the insulted and injured but may drive him to compensate for what he misses by realizing and developing is capacities and talents.

About the Author

ERIC HOFFER works three days each week as a longshoreman in San Francisco and spends one day as "research professor" at the University of California in Berkeley.

Of his early life Mr. Hoffer has written: "I had no schooling. I was practically blind up to the age of fifteen. When my eyesight came back I was seized with an enormous hunger for the printed word. I read indiscriminately everything within reach—English and German.

"When my father (a cabinet-maker) died I realized that I would have to fend for myself. I knew several things: One, that I didn't want to work in a factory; two, that I couldn't stand being dependent on the good graces of a boss; three, that I was going to stay poor; four, that I had to get out of New York. Logic told me that California was the poor man's country."

Through ten years as a migratory fieldworker on the West Coast and as a gold-miner around Nevada City Mr. Hoffer worked long and hard, but continued to read and to scribble. These were the years of depression. The Okies and the Arkies were the "new pioneers," and Mr. Hoffer was one of them. He had library cards in a dozen towns along the railroad, and when he was in pocket he took a room near a library for concentrated thinking and writing. Out of these experiences developed his interest in the common man, mass movements and those social and economic forces that shape our history.

In 1943 Mr. Hoffer chose the longshoreman's life and settled in California. He has since written four books: *The True Believer, The Passionate State of Mind, The Ordeal of Change* and *The Temper of Our Time.* During the 1964-1965 season he was the subject of twelve half-hour programs on National Educational Television.

Design by Ellen H. Brecher
Set in Times Roman
Composed, printed and bound by The Colonial Press, Inc.
HARPER & ROW, PUBLISHERS, INCORPORATED